WHAT ARE THE WORLD RELIGIONS?

Kids' Guides to God's Word Series

What Is the Book of Genesis?
What Is the Book of Exodus?
What Is the Book of Leviticus?
What Is the Book of Numbers?
What Is the Book of Deuteronomy?
What Is the Book of Joshua?
What Is the Book of Judges?
What Is the Book of Ruth?
What Is the Book of 1 Samuel?
What Is the Book of 2 Samuel?
What Is the Book of 1 Kings?
What Is the Book of 2 Kings?
What Are the Books of 1–2 Chronicles?
What Are the Books of Ezra & Nehemiah?
What Is the Book of Esther?
What Is the Book of Job?
What Is the Book of Psalms?
What Is the Book of Proverbs?
What Is the Book of Ecclesiastes?
What Are the Books of Song of Songs & Lamentations?
What Is the Book of Isaiah?
What Is the Book of Jeremiah?
What Is the Book of Ezekiel?
What Is the Book of Daniel?
What Are the Books of Hosea–Micah?
What Are the Books of Nahum–Malachi?
What Is the Gospel of Matthew?
What Is the Gospel of Mark?
What Is the Gospel of Luke?
What Is the Gospel of John?
What Is the Book of Acts?
What Is the Book of Romans?
What Is the Book of 1 Corinthians?
What Is the Book of 2 Corinthians?
What Is the Book of Galatians?
What Is the Book of Ephesians?
What Is the Book of Philippians?
What Are the Books of Colossians & Philemon?
What Are the Books of 1–2 Thessalonians?
What Are the Books of 1–2 Timothy & Titus?
What Is the Book of Hebrews?
What Is the Book of James?
What Are the Books of 1–2 Peter & Jude?
What Are the Books of 1-3 John?
What Is the Book of Revelation?

What Are the

WORLD RELIGIONS?

Michael Whitworth

ISBN 978-1-971767-44-4

Published by Start2Finish
Bend, Oregon 97702
start2finish.org

Printed in the United States of America

30 29 28 27 26 1 2 3 4 5

CONTENTS

INTRODUCTION

Picture the first day at a new school. You walk through the front doors and immediately notice that not everyone talks the way you do. Some kids greet each other in languages you have never heard. The lunchroom smells different from what you are used to. Someone in your class wears a head covering. Someone else has a red dot on their forehead. A kid at the locker next to yours mentions that he cannot eat until sundown because his family is fasting. You smile and nod, but inside you are thinking, *What is going on?*

That moment is not imaginary. It is happening in schools, neighborhoods, and workplaces all over the world, every single day. The planet has gotten smaller. The people in your life come from more backgrounds and believe more different things than at any other point in history. And whether you are ready for it or not, you are going to have conversations about what people believe and why.

This book exists to help you be ready.

WHY THIS BOOK MATTERS

Here is a truth that might surprise you: studying other religions is not dangerous. It is necessary. Some Christians are afraid that learning about other faiths will shake their own. But the opposite is usually true. The more clearly you understand what others believe, the more clearly you see what makes the gospel of Jesus unique.

Think of it this way. A jeweler does not learn to spot a counterfeit diamond by avoiding diamonds. She studies the real thing so carefully that the fakes become obvious by comparison. That is what this book is designed to do. Every chapter will help you understand another worldview on its own terms, and every chapter will bring you back to the Bible so you can see the differences for yourself.

This is not a book about winning arguments. It is a book about understanding people. The world is full of Hindus, Buddhists, Muslims, Sikhs, and others who are not cartoon villains. They are real people, made in the image of God, who hold their beliefs with the same sincerity you hold yours. You can disagree with someone's theology and still treat them with dignity. In fact, that is exactly what Jesus expects you to do.

WHAT YOU ARE ABOUT TO READ

This book covers some of the world's most significant religious traditions, organized in a deliberate order.

Chapter 1 lays the foundation by walking through the core beliefs and practices of Christianity as taught in the New Testament. This is your home base. Everything that follows is measured against it.

From there, the book moves outward in circles. Chapter 2 examines Catholicism, a tradition that shares Christianity's core creeds but adds layers of authority and practice that go beyond what Scripture teaches. Chapter 3 looks at Mormonism and the Jehovah's Witnesses, groups that use Christian language but have rewritten the story in fundamental ways.

Chapters 4–5 cover Judaism and Islam, the two other faiths that trace their roots back to Abraham. Both worship one God, and both share parts of the biblical story, but each takes a dramatically different turn when it comes to Jesus.

Chapters 6–9 move further from familiar territory. Hinduism introduces a world of many gods, karma, and reincarnation. Buddhism offers a path to escape suffering without any god at all. Chinese traditional religion blends multiple systems into a single cultural practice. And Sikhism presents a form of monotheism that grew out of the Indian subcontinent with its own distinct identity.

Each chapter follows the same pattern. You will find an opening illustration to draw you in, a careful explanation of what the religion teaches, a comparison to biblical Christianity, four application points under "What This Means for Us," and five discussion questions under "Talking Points." The structure is the same every time so that you can focus on the content rather than figuring out where you are.

BEFORE YOU START

There are a few things to keep in mind as you read.

First, be honest. If something in another religion sounds appealing, do not pretend it does not. Confucian respect for parents is admirable. Sikh generosity is inspiring. Buddhist honesty about suffering is refreshing. Acknowledging what is good in another tradition does not weaken your faith. It shows that you are paying attention.

Second, be fair. Every religion in this book is summarized in a single chapter, which means every religion in this book is simplified. Entire libraries have been written about Hinduism, Islam, and Buddhism. One chapter cannot capture every detail or every perspective within a tradition. This book will give you an honest and accurate starting point, but it is a starting point, not the final word.

Third, be confident. You do not need to be nervous about what you are going to find. The gospel has been tested by sharper critics than you, and that's not meant to be insulting. God's word has survived two thousand years of challenges, and it is not going to crumble because you learned what the Buddha taught about suffering. Confidence in the truth does not require ignorance of everything else.

Fourth, be kind. The goal of this book is not to arm you for battle against your neighbors. It is to equip you for conversation with them. The people who follow these religions are not your enemies. Many of them are searching for the same things you are: meaning, hope, belonging, and answers to the questions that keep everyone up at night. When you know what they believe and why, you are better positioned to share what you believe with clarity and compassion.

The apostle Peter wrote, "In your hearts honor Christ the Lord as holy, always being prepared to make a defense to anyone who asks you for a reason for the hope that is in you; yet do it with gentleness and respect" (1 Peter 3:15). That verse is the mission statement for this entire book. Be prepared. Be clear. And be kind.

Turn the page.

1

NEW TESTAMENT CHRISTIANITY

Have you ever tried to give someone directions to your house? You probably start with a landmark they already know, like a school or a gas station, and then walk them through the turns from there. But here is the thing: you can only give those directions because *you* already know where your house is. If you did not know your own address, every set of directions in the world would be useless to you.

This book is going to take you on a tour of the world's major religions. You will visit synagogues and mosques, temples and shrines. You will meet prophets, gurus, and monks. Some of what you discover will sound strange, and some of it will sound surprisingly familiar. But before you can understand how other religions compare to Christianity, you need to know Christianity itself. Not just the bumper-sticker version. Not just "Jesus loves me, this I know." You need to understand what Christians believe, why they believe it, and how those beliefs shape the way they live every single day.

Think of this chapter as your home address. Once you know it by heart, you will be able to navigate everything that comes next.

ONE GOD

Christianity begins with a bold and simple claim: there is one God. Not dozens. Not thousands. One. "Hear, O Israel: The LORD our God, the LORD is one" (Deuteronomy 6:4). That verse was the cornerstone of Israel's faith for centuries before Jesus was born, and it is still the foundation of Christianity today.

But Christians believe something that surprises a lot of people: this one God exists as three persons. God the Father, God the Son (Jesus), and God the Holy Spirit are each fully God, yet there are not three gods. There is one. Christians call this the Trinity, and if it sounds hard to wrap your brain around, you are in good company. Believers have been wrestling with this truth for two thousand years. It is not a puzzle to be solved so much as a reality to be respected. The Bible does not use the word "Trinity," but the idea runs all through its pages, from the Spirit hovering over the waters at creation (Genesis 1:2) to Jesus commanding his followers to baptize "in the name of the Father and of the Son and of the Holy Spirit" (Matthew 28:19).

Why does this matter? Because the God of Christianity is not a distant force or an impersonal energy. He is a God who exists in relationship, and he invites people into that relationship.

THE BIBLE

Every religion has its sacred texts, and for Christians that text is the Bible. It is actually a library of sixty-six books written by dozens of authors over roughly 1,500 years. It includes history, poetry, prophecy, letters, and law. The first thirty-nine books make up the Old Testament, which tells the story of

God creating the world, calling a people (Israel), and making promises that would not be fully kept until Jesus arrived. The last twenty-seven books make up the New Testament, which records the life of Jesus, the birth of the church, and instructions for how to follow God until Jesus returns.

New Testament Christians hold a conviction that makes them distinct from many other groups: the Bible alone is the authority for faith and practice. There is no creed book, no catechism, and no church council that gets the final word. If a belief or practice cannot be supported by Scripture, it has no place in the life of the church. That does not mean Christians agree on every detail, but it does mean the Bible is always the standard they come back to when there is a disagreement.

This principle will come up again and again as you read through this book. When you look at other religions, one of the first questions to ask is always: *Where does the authority come from?*

THE PROBLEM

Here is where the story takes a turn that nobody likes but everybody recognizes. Something is wrong with the world, and something is wrong with us. The Bible calls it sin.

Sin is not just breaking rules. It is a broken relationship. When the first humans, Adam and Eve, chose to disobey God in the garden of Eden, they introduced a fracture into creation that has never healed on its own. Every lie you have told, every unkind word you have spoken, every selfish choice you have made is proof that the fracture runs through you, too. "For all have sinned and fall short of the glory of God" (Romans 3:23). That verse does not leave anyone out. All means all.

The consequences of sin are serious. "For the wages of sin is death" (Romans 6:23). Not just physical death, though that is part of it. The Bible describes an eternal separation from God that awaits those who die without being reconciled to him. That sounds heavy, and it should. Christianity does not sugarcoat the problem. But it does offer a solution that changes everything.

THE SOLUTION

The solution has a name: Jesus. Christians believe that Jesus of Nazareth was not simply a good teacher or an inspiring leader. He was God in the flesh. The Son of God left heaven, was born to a virgin named Mary, and lived a fully human life without ever sinning. That last part is important, because it means he was the only person in history who did not deserve death. And yet he died anyway.

Around AD 30, Jesus was arrested on false charges, beaten, and nailed to a Roman cross outside the city of Jerusalem. He died and was buried in a borrowed tomb. But three days later, the tomb was empty. Jesus rose from the dead, appeared to hundreds of witnesses over the course of forty days, and then ascended into heaven where he sits at the right hand of God the Father.

Why did all of this happen? Because God loved the world too much to leave it broken. "For God so loved the world, that he gave his only Son, that whoever believes in him should not perish but have eternal life" (John 3:16). The cross was not an accident or a tragedy. It was a rescue mission. Jesus took the punishment for sin that every human being deserved, and his resurrection proved that death itself had been defeated.

This is the heart of Christianity. Everything else flows from this one event.

RESPONDING TO THE GOOD NEWS

If Jesus did all the work, does that mean people just sit back and accept it? Not exactly. The Bible teaches that salvation is a gift of grace. No one can earn it. But a gift still has to be received, and the New Testament is clear about how that happens.

It starts with *hearing* the good news about Jesus. "So faith comes from hearing, and hearing through the word of Christ" (Romans 10:17). You cannot respond to a message you have never encountered.

Next comes *believing*. Not just believing that God exists, but trusting that Jesus is who he claimed to be and that his death and resurrection actually accomplished what God said they would. "Without faith it is impossible to please God" (Hebrews 11:6).

Belief leads to *repentance*, which means turning your life in a new direction. On the day the church was born, the apostle Peter told a crowd of convicted listeners, "Repent and be baptized every one of you in the name of Jesus Christ for the forgiveness of your sins" (Acts 2:38). Repentance is not just feeling sorry; it is making a decision to change.

Then comes *confession*. Romans 10:9 says, "If you confess with your mouth that Jesus is Lord and believe in your heart that God raised him from the dead, you will be saved." Confession is going public with your faith. It is telling the world whose side you are on.

Finally, a believer is *baptized*. Baptism is an immersion in water for the forgiveness of sins. It is not an empty ritual or an optional add-on. It is the moment when a person is united with Christ in his death, burial, and resurrection (Romans 6:3–4). When you come up out of that water, you come up as a new creation.

Does this sequence of steps earn salvation? No. Salvation is still a gift from start to finish. But these are the ways God has told us to receive that gift, and trusting him enough to do what he says is what faith looks like in action.

THE CHURCH

When someone is baptized into Christ, they are added to his church. Not a denomination. Not a building. The church is the body of Christ, a living community of people who belong to him.

In the New Testament, each local church was led by a group of men called elders or shepherds. These were not distant executives running things from an office. They were mature Christian men who lived among the congregation and cared for it the way a shepherd cares for sheep. Churches also had deacons, who served practical needs, and preachers or evangelists, who taught and spread the gospel. There was no pope, no president, and no central headquarters. Each congregation answered directly to Christ through his word.

The churches of Christ today try to follow that same pattern. You will not find a denominational structure or a human creed. The goal is simple: be the church you read about in the New Testament. That does not mean every congregation is perfect, but it does mean there is a constant effort to measure everything against Scripture.

WORSHIP

If you walked into a church of Christ on a Sunday morning, you would notice a few things right away.

First, you would hear singing, but you would not see a band. Churches of Christ practice what is called a cappella worship, meaning they sing without instruments. This is not because they dislike music. It is because the New Testament instructions for worship mention singing (Ephesians 5:19; Colossians 3:16) but never mention instruments, and the churches of Christ take seriously the principle of doing what Scripture authorizes rather than adding to it.

Second, you would see the Lord's Supper served every Sunday. This is a simple meal of unleavened bread and grape juice that represents the body and blood of Jesus. The early church observed it on the first day of every week (Acts 20:7), and churches of Christ continue that practice today. It is a weekly reminder of Jesus' death on the cross and the cost of salvation.

You would also hear prayers offered to God, a sermon from the Scriptures, and a collection taken to support the work of the church. None of it is flashy. The focus is not on entertaining the audience but on honoring God and encouraging his people.

THE HOPE AHEAD

Christianity is not just about the past. It is also about the future. Jesus promised that one day he would return. When he does, the dead will be raised, and everyone who has ever lived will stand before God in judgment. Those who belong to Christ will receive eternal life. Those who rejected him will face eternal separation from God.

Christians also believe in the resurrection of the body. The hope is not simply that your soul floats away to some cloudy spiritual realm. It is that God will make all things new, including you. Just as Jesus rose from the dead in a physical body, those who belong to him will be raised to live forever in a new creation where sin, suffering, and death are finally gone for good.

That hope shapes how Christians live right now. It gives courage in the face of suffering, generosity in the face of need, and purpose in the face of the ordinary. If death is not the end, then nothing you do for God is ever wasted.

WHAT THIS MEANS FOR US

First, know what you believe before you compare. You would never take a test without studying, and you should never evaluate another religion without first understanding your own. The better you know the Bible and the gospel, the better equipped you will be to spot what is true and what is not when you encounter other belief systems.

Second, authority matters more than feelings. Every religion claims to offer truth, but not every religion agrees on where truth comes from. Christianity's answer is the Bible. When you evaluate any religious teaching, the first question to ask is: *Where is the evidence for this?* If the answer is a feeling, a tradition, or a human teacher's opinion, that is very different from "the Bible says."

Third, grace changes the equation. Most religions in this book will describe some version of earning your way to God. Christianity stands apart because it insists the opposite is true. You cannot earn what Jesus offers. You can only receive it. That single idea will look more and more remarkable the further you read.

Fourth, the church is the plan. God did not save people and then leave them to figure out the rest alone. He placed them in a community designed to help them grow, serve, and stay faithful. If you are a Christian, the church is not an accessory to your faith. It is part of the design.

TALKING POINTS

1. Why is it important to understand your own faith deeply before studying what others believe? What could go wrong if you skipped that step?

2. The chapter describes the Bible as the sole authority for faith and practice. Why do you think some groups have added other sources of authority alongside (or above) the Bible? What problems might that create?

3. Christianity teaches that salvation is a gift of grace, not something earned. Why do you think so many people still feel like they need to earn God's approval? Have you ever felt that way?

4. What would you say to someone who argued that baptism is not really necessary and that believing in Jesus is all that matters?

5. If a friend from another religion asked you to explain what Christians believe in just two or three sentences, what would you say?

Christianity is not complicated, but it is complete. One God created you, loved you enough to rescue you through his Son, and gave you a place in his family called the church. The Bible tells that story from beginning to end, and it is the measuring stick for everything that follows in this book.

Now that you know your home address, it is time to start exploring. In the chapters ahead, you will encounter faiths that borrow pieces of this story, faiths that rewrite it, and faiths that tell an entirely different story altogether. Keep what you have learned here close, because it will be your guide for every stop along the way.

Turn the page.

2

CATHOLICISM

Jonathan Swift's famous novel *Gulliver's Travels* introduces readers to the tiny people of Lilliput, who are locked in a bitter war with their neighbors, the Blefuscudians. The cause of the conflict? Eggs. Specifically, which end of a boiled egg should be cracked open. The Big-Endians insist on cracking the large end. The Little-Endians demand the small end. The disagreement has sparked six rebellions, cost thousands of lives, and divided an entire civilization. The whole time, the reader is shaking their head because both sides are fighting over *an egg*.

Swift wrote that story as a satire, poking fun at real religious and political arguments in his own day. And while it is tempting to laugh at the Lilliputians, his point hits close to home. Sometimes groups that agree on almost everything end up in an enormous fight over the things they do not.

That brings us to Catholicism.

Of all the religions you will encounter in this book, Catholicism shares the most common ground with what you learned in Chapter 1. Catholics believe in the same God, read the same Bible (with a few additional books), confess the same creeds about Jesus, and worship on the same day. This is not a Lilliputian egg war. Catholics are not enemies, and the differences are not silly. But the differences are real, and they matter more than you might expect. Understanding where and why the road forks will sharpen your understanding of what the Bible actually teaches.

WHAT WE SHARE

Before we talk about the differences, it is only fair to start with what Catholicism and New Testament Christianity have in common, because the list is longer than most people realize.

Catholics believe in one God who exists as the Trinity: Father, Son, and Holy Spirit. They believe Jesus is the Son of God, born of a virgin, fully God and fully human. They believe he died on the cross for sin, rose from the dead on the third day, and ascended to heaven. They believe he is coming back. They believe the Bible is the inspired word of God. They practice baptism and the Lord's Supper. They believe in a final judgment and eternal life.

That is not a small amount of shared ground. On the biggest questions of all, who is God and who is Jesus, Catholics and New Testament Christians stand on the same side of the line. When you compare this chapter to the ones on Hinduism or Buddhism later in the book, the distance between Catholicism and New Testament Christians will look like a crack in the sidewalk next to the Grand Canyon.

But cracks in the sidewalk can still trip you up, especially if you do not see them coming.

THE QUESTION OF AUTHORITY

The most important difference between Catholicism and New Testament Christians is not about any single belief. It is about how beliefs are decided in the first place.

In Chapter 1, you learned that New Testament Christians look to the Bible alone as the authority for faith and practice. If the Bible teaches it, we follow it. If the Bible is silent on it, we do not bind it. The goal is to let Scripture be the final word.

Catholicism takes a different approach. The Catholic Church teaches that there are *three* sources of authority: Scripture, Sacred Tradition, and the Magisterium (the official teaching authority of the church, led by the Pope and the bishops). In this system, the Bible is important, but it does not stand alone. The traditions passed down through centuries of church history carry real weight, and the Pope has the authority to interpret both the Bible and those traditions in a way that is binding on all Catholics.

This difference might sound like a technical detail, but it is actually the root of almost every other disagreement. Once you add tradition and a human leader as sources of authority alongside Scripture, the door is open for teachings that cannot be found in the Bible at all. And that is exactly what has happened over the centuries.

THE POPE

The Catholic Church is led by the Pope, who is considered the head of the church on earth. Catholics believe the Pope is the successor of the apostle Peter, and they point to Matthew 16:18 as the basis for this claim. In that verse, Jesus says to Peter, "On this rock I will build my church." Catholics interpret this to mean that Peter was given unique authority over the church, and that this authority has been passed down through an unbroken chain of leaders all the way to the current Pope.

New Testament Christians read that passage differently. The "rock" Jesus referred to was not Peter himself but Peter's confession that Jesus is "the Christ, the Son of the living God" (Matthew 16:16). The foundation of the church is not a man. It is the truth about who Jesus is.

Beyond that, the New Testament simply does not describe the kind of structure that the Catholic Church has built. You will not find a single leader with authority over all congregations. What you find instead is a pattern of local churches, each led by their own elders, answering to Christ. The apostle Peter himself wrote to elders and told them to "shepherd the flock of God that is among you" (1 Peter 5:2), not to hand their authority over to a central leader.

The Catholic system also teaches that when the Pope speaks on matters of faith and morals in his official capacity, he is infallible. That means he cannot be wrong. This teaching was officially declared in 1870 and is one of the clearest examples of how tradition and church authority can produce beliefs that have no basis in Scripture.

SACRED TRADITION

The Catholic Church teaches that not everything God revealed was written down in the Bible. Some truths, they say, were passed along orally through the apostles and preserved in the traditions of the church. These traditions are given the same weight as Scripture.

The problem is that many of these traditions teach things the Bible never mentions, and in some cases they teach things that seem to contradict the Bible entirely. Where do teachings like purgatory, the rosary, or praying to saints come from? They do not come from Genesis through Revelation. They come from traditions that developed over centuries, and they were eventually accepted as official church teaching because the Catholic system allows tradition to function as a second Bible.

The apostle Paul warned the Colossians, "See to it that no one takes you captive by philosophy and empty deceit, according to human tradition" (Colossians 2:8). That verse does not mean all tradition is bad. But it does mean that tradition is not automatically true just because it has been around a long time. Everything must be tested against Scripture.

MARY AND THE SAINTS

One of the most visible differences between Catholicism and New Testament Christianity involves Mary, the mother of Jesus. Catholics hold Mary in extraordinarily high regard. The church teaches that Mary was conceived without original sin, that she remained a virgin her entire life, and that at the end of her earthly life she was taken bodily into heaven. Catholics also pray to Mary, asking her to intercede with God on their behalf.

None of these teachings appear in the New Testament. The Bible honors Mary as a faithful woman who was chosen for an incredible role, and there is no reason to take anything away from that. But the Bible also mentions Jesus' brothers

(Matthew 13:55), which challenges the claim of her perpetual virginity. More importantly, the Bible never instructs anyone to pray to Mary or to any other human being who has died.

This extends to the Catholic practice of praying to saints. Catholics believe that holy men and women who have died can hear prayers and bring those requests to God. New Testament Christians see a problem with this. The Bible says there is "one mediator between God and men, the man Christ Jesus" (1 Timothy 2:5). Prayer is directed to God through Jesus Christ. Adding anyone else to that line of communication is not something Scripture supports.

Catholics would be quick to point out that they are not worshiping Mary or the saints. They make a distinction between worship, which belongs to God alone, and veneration, which is a special honor. That distinction makes sense on paper, but in practice it can become very difficult to tell the difference, especially when statues are bowed before and prayers are directed to someone other than God.

SALVATION

Both Catholics and New Testament Christians believe that salvation comes through Jesus Christ. But the two groups have different understandings of how salvation works and how it is received.

Catholic teaching describes salvation as a process that involves faith, good works, and participation in the seven sacraments (Baptism, Confirmation, Eucharist, Reconciliation, Anointing of the Sick, Holy Orders, and Matrimony). Grace flows to the believer primarily through these sacraments, which must be administered by ordained priests. The system is detailed and structured, with each sacrament playing a specific role in the believer's spiritual life.

But you can find a much simpler picture of salvation in the New Testament. As you read in Chapter 1, the gospel calls for hearing, believing, repenting, confessing, and being baptized. There is no priestly class required to administer grace. There are no extra sacraments beyond what Scripture describes. The Lord's Supper and baptism are two practices clearly established in the New Testament, and neither one requires a specially ordained person to oversee them.

Catholicism also teaches the existence of purgatory, a place where the souls of believers are purified after death before entering heaven. The idea is that most people, even faithful ones, are not quite ready for heaven when they die and need additional cleansing. New Testament Christians reject this teaching because it appears nowhere in Scripture. The Bible speaks of heaven and hell, of life and death, but never of a middle stop along the way. The thief on the cross was told by Jesus, "Today you will be with me in paradise" (Luke 23:43). There was no mention of waiting or purification.

WORSHIP AND PRACTICE

Some of the most noticeable differences between Catholicism and New Testament Christianity show up in worship.

Catholic worship centers on the Mass, an elaborate service that follows a set liturgy, or script, each week. The highlight of the Mass is the Eucharist, in which the priest consecrates bread and wine that Catholics believe literally become the body and blood of Christ. This teaching is called transubstantiation, and it has been a core Catholic belief since the Middle Ages. New Testament Christians observe the Lord's Supper each Sunday as well, but they understand the bread and fruit of the vine as symbols that represent the body and blood of Jesus, not as his literal flesh and blood.

Catholic worship also includes instrumental music, choirs, incense, and a variety of rituals and ceremonies that have developed over the centuries. As you read in Chapter 1, New Testament Christians sing without instruments, aiming to follow the New Testament pattern as closely as possible.

Another major difference is the priesthood. In Catholicism, ordained priests serve as mediators between the people and God. They hear confessions, perform sacraments, and are considered essential to the spiritual life of the church. The New Testament, however, teaches the priesthood of all believers (1 Peter 2:9). Every Christian has direct access to God through Jesus. There is no special class of people required to stand between you and your Creator.

A FAMILY DISAGREEMENT

It is important to keep perspective here. Catholics love God, study the Bible, serve their communities, and follow Jesus with sincere hearts. Many of the greatest hospitals, universities, and charitable organizations in the world were built by Catholics.

But love and sincerity do not settle the question of whether a teaching is biblical. A person can be completely sincere and still be mistaken. New Testament Christians believe that the safest path is the one that stays closest to what the Bible actually says, without adding layers of tradition and human authority on top of it. When you strip away the centuries of added tradition, the Christianity that remains looks a lot like what you read in the New Testament: simple, direct, and anchored to the word of God.

That is not an insult to Catholics. It is an invitation to everyone to go back to the source and see what it says.

WHAT THIS MEANS FOR US

First, common ground is real ground. It is easy to focus so much on differences that you forget how much you share with Catholic believers. They worship the same God, trust the same Savior, and read the same Scriptures. When you talk with a Catholic friend, start with what unites you before you get to what divides you.

Second, authority is the real issue. Almost every specific disagreement between Catholicism and New Testament Christians traces back to the question of authority. If you settle that question by going to Scripture alone, most of the other questions answer themselves.

Third, tradition is not automatically wrong, but it is not automatically right either. Some traditions are helpful. Some are harmless. But the moment a tradition is treated as equal to Scripture, it has been given a power it was never meant to have (see Matthew 15:9). Always ask: *Where does the Bible teach this?*

Fourth, respect the people even when you question the teaching. Catholics are not your enemies. They are people made in the image of God, and many of them have a deep, genuine faith. Disagreeing with someone's theology does not give you permission to be unkind. The goal is truth and love together, not one without the other.

TALKING POINTS

1. What surprised you most about the things Catholicism and New Testament Christianity have in common? Did you expect the shared ground to be that large?

2. Why is the question of authority (Bible alone vs. Bible plus tradition plus the Pope) such a big deal? How does it affect what a church ends up believing and practicing?

3. Catholics make a distinction between worshiping God and venerating Mary and the saints. Do you think that distinction is clear enough in practice? Why or why not?

4. The chapter mentions that the thief on the cross went straight to paradise with no mention of purgatory. What does that tell you about what happens after death for those who trust in Jesus?

5. How can you disagree with a friend's religious beliefs without making them feel attacked or disrespected? What does that kind of conversation look like?

Catholicism and New Testament Christianity are closer to each other than either group is to any other religion in this book. That closeness is exactly why the differences deserve careful attention. When two things look almost the same, the details that set them apart matter all the more. As you continue through the chapters ahead, you will find that the question you learned here—"Where does the Bible teach this?"—is the single most useful tool in your kit. Keep it close.

Turn the page.

3

MORMONISM & JEHOVAH'S WITNESSES

The movie *Catch Me If You Can* tells the story of Frank Abagnale Jr., a teenager who ran away from home in the 1960s and pulled off one of the most audacious cons in American history. Frank did not rob banks with a mask and a gun. He did something far more clever. He dressed up as a Pan Am airline pilot, complete with the uniform, the badge, and the confident walk. Airlines let him into cockpits. Hotels gave him free rooms. Banks cashed his forged checks without blinking. Later, he posed as a doctor and even a lawyer, passing himself off so convincingly that the people around him never questioned whether he was the real thing.

What made Frank so effective was not that he invented something new. It was that he borrowed something familiar. He used real uniforms, real titles, and real language. Everything on the outside looked exactly right. But underneath the surface, the truth was missing entirely.

That same pattern shows up in the world of religion. Some groups use Christian vocabulary, carry Christian-looking scriptures, and knock on your door talking about Jesus.

They look and sound like they belong to the same faith you read about in Chapter 1. But when you look underneath the surface, the God they describe, the Jesus they follow, and the gospel they teach have been quietly replaced with something very different. Two of the most well-known groups that fit this description are the Church of Jesus Christ of Latter-day Saints (commonly called Mormons) and the Jehovah's Witnesses.

THE MORMONS: A NEW STORY

The Church of Jesus Christ of Latter-day Saints was founded by a man named Joseph Smith in upstate New York in 1830. Smith claimed that when he was fourteen years old, God the Father and Jesus Christ appeared to him in a vision and told him that every church on earth had fallen into error. According to Smith, God had chosen him to restore true Christianity.

A few years later, Smith said an angel named Moroni directed him to a set of golden plates buried in a hillside. Smith translated these plates, and the result was the Book of Mormon, which Mormons treat as Scripture alongside the Bible. But the Book of Mormon is not the only text they have added. Mormons also accept the Doctrine and Covenants and the Pearl of Great Price as inspired writings. So while Mormons say they believe the Bible, in practice it is just one book among several, and when the Bible conflicts with their other scriptures, it is the Bible that usually gets set aside.

This matters because what the Bible teaches and what these additional books teach are not the same thing.

A DIFFERENT GOD

The most serious departure in Mormon teaching is what it says about God himself.

Christianity teaches that God is eternal, unchanging, and spirit. He has always been God and always will be. The Mormon view is dramatically different. Mormon theology teaches that God the Father was once a human being on another planet who lived a mortal life, died, and eventually progressed to godhood. Even more startling, Mormons believe that faithful human beings can follow the same path and become gods themselves one day, ruling over their own worlds.

This is not a minor disagreement about a footnote. It is a completely different understanding of who God is. The Bible says, "Before me no god was formed, nor shall there be any after me" (Isaiah 43:10). God is not a promoted human. He is the Creator of everything, and there is no one like him.

Mormon teaching also rejects the Trinity. Rather than one God in three persons, Mormons believe the Father, Son, and Holy Spirit are three separate gods who happen to be united in purpose. They teach that God the Father has a physical body of flesh and bone. The Bible contradicts this directly: "God is spirit" (John 4:24).

A DIFFERENT JESUS

Because Mormonism has a different view of God, it also has a different view of Jesus. Mormon theology teaches that Jesus was the firstborn spirit child of God the Father and a heavenly mother. It also teaches that Lucifer (Satan) was another spirit child of the same father, making Jesus and Satan spirit brothers.

Nothing in the Bible remotely supports this idea. Scripture teaches that Jesus is God (John 1:1), that he created all things (Colossians 1:16), and that he existed with the Father before anything was made. He is not a created being and he is certainly not the brother of the devil. The Jesus described in Mormon theology may share a name with the Jesus of the Bible, but the two are not the same person.

MORMON PRACTICES

Several Mormon practices have no basis in Scripture. One of the most unusual is baptism for the dead. Mormons believe that living people can be baptized on behalf of relatives who died without hearing the Mormon gospel. They base this on a single verse, 1 Corinthians 15:29, but that verse is one of the most debated passages in the entire New Testament, and Paul does not endorse the practice. He simply mentions that some people were doing it as part of a larger argument about the resurrection.

Mormons also practice temple rituals that are closed to outsiders, including ceremonies for marriage that they believe seal families together for eternity. These rituals have no connection to anything described in the New Testament.

The Mormon church is led by a president who is considered a living prophet, along with twelve apostles. This leadership structure claims direct authority from God, and members are expected to follow their guidance. Questioning the prophet is strongly discouraged. Once again, a human institution has placed itself between the believer and God's word.

THE JEHOVAH'S WITNESSES: A REWRITTEN BIBLE

The Jehovah's Witnesses were founded in the 1870s by a man named Charles Taze Russell in Pennsylvania. Russell began as a Bible study leader, but his teachings gradually moved further and further from what Scripture actually says. Today the organization is headquartered in New York and is led by a small group of men called the Governing Body, who claim to be God's sole channel of communication with the world.

Unlike the Mormons, the Jehovah's Witnesses did not add new books to the Bible. Instead, they produced their own translation of the Bible, called the New World Translation. This translation changes key verses in ways that support Jehovah's Witness theology. The most famous example is John 1:1. Most English translations read, "The Word was God." The New World Translation changes this to, "The Word was *a* god," with a lowercase "g." That single word change turns Jesus from being God into being a lesser, created being. It is not an honest translation of the original text. It is a rewrite designed to match a conclusion they had already reached.

A DIFFERENT JESUS (AGAIN)

Like the Mormons, the Jehovah's Witnesses reject the Trinity. They believe that Jehovah (their preferred name for God) is the only true God and that Jesus is a created being. Specifically, they teach that Jesus is actually Michael the archangel, the first being God ever created, who later came to earth in human form.

The Bible does not support this. Hebrews 1:5 asks, "To which of the angels did God ever say, 'You are my Son'?" The entire first chapter of Hebrews is built around the argument that Jesus is greater than the angels. Calling Jesus an angel is not just a small mistake. It strips him of his deity and makes the cross something less than what it is.

Jehovah's Witnesses also reject the idea that the Holy Spirit is a person. They describe the Spirit as God's "active force," more like electricity than a being. But the Bible describes the Holy Spirit using personal language: the Spirit speaks (Acts 13:2), can be lied to (Acts 5:3), and can be grieved (Ephesians 4:30). Forces do not grieve. Persons do.

SALVATION AND THE AFTERLIFE

Jehovah's Witness teaching about salvation looks very different from what the New Testament describes.

They teach that only 144,000 people will ever go to heaven. This number comes from Revelation 7 and 14, but those passages are part of a highly symbolic book, and there is no reason to take that specific number as a literal headcount while treating the rest of the images in Revelation as symbolic. According to their teaching, the vast majority of faithful Jehovah's Witnesses will not go to heaven at all. Instead, they will live forever on a paradise earth after God destroys the wicked.

They also reject the existence of hell. They teach that the wicked will simply be annihilated, meaning they will cease to exist. On the contrary, the New Testament describes eternal separation from God as a conscious reality (Matthew 25:46).

Salvation for a Jehovah's Witness is also heavily tied to the organization itself. Being part of the Watchtower organization is considered essential. Those who leave or are expelled (a process called disfellowshipping) are shunned by their families and former friends. This practice creates enormous pressure to stay, even for those who have serious doubts.

FAILED PREDICTIONS

One of the most damaging aspects of Jehovah's Witness history is their record of false predictions. The organization has repeatedly set dates for the end of the world or the return of Christ: 1914, 1925, and 1975 are among the most well-known examples. When those dates came and went without the promised events, the organization either quietly adjusted the timeline or reinterpreted what the prediction was supposed to mean.

The Bible is blunt about this kind of thing. Deuteronomy 18:22 says, "When a prophet speaks in the name of the LORD, if the word does not come to pass or come true, that is a word that the LORD has not spoken." A track record of false predictions does not inspire confidence that an organization is speaking for God.

WHAT THEY HAVE IN COMMON

Mormonism and the Jehovah's Witnesses are very different from each other in many ways, but they share several patterns that are worth noticing.

Both groups claim to be the only true restoration of Christianity. Both were founded by individuals who claimed special authority from God. Both have added to or altered the text of Scripture to fit their own teachings. Both reject the Trinity and teach a version of Jesus that is less than what the Bible describes. And both are led by centralized human authorities who discourage independent study of the Bible outside their approved materials.

That last point is especially important. In churches that belong to Jesus Christ, you are encouraged to open your Bible, read it for yourself, and come to your own conclusions based on what the text says. Any group that discourages that kind of open study is a group that is afraid of what you might find.

WHY THIS CHAPTER MATTERS

You may wonder why Mormonism and the Jehovah's Witnesses get their own chapter instead of being grouped with Hinduism or Buddhism later in the book. The reason is simple: these groups are far more likely to show up at your front door. Mormon missionaries are some of the most active in the world. Jehovah's Witnesses are known for their door-to-door visits. Both groups will use familiar Christian language, quote Bible verses, and present themselves as fellow believers.

If you do not know what the Bible actually teaches, it is easy to be caught off guard. But if you have done your homework, you will be able to recognize when a familiar word is being used with an unfamiliar meaning. And you will be able to respond, not with hostility, but with grace and truth.

WHAT THIS MEANS FOR US

First, same words do not always mean the same thing. Mormons and Jehovah's Witnesses both talk about God, Jesus, salvation, and the Bible. But they have redefined every one of those words. When someone claims to be Christian, the question to ask is not just *what words do you use?* but *what do you mean by them?*

Second, the Bible does not need an upgrade. Both groups either added new scriptures or rewrote the ones that already exist. The Bible claims to be complete and sufficient. "All Scripture is breathed out by God and profitable for teaching" (2 Timothy 3:16). If someone tells you the Bible is not enough, that should raise a red flag immediately.

Third, test everything. The apostle John wrote, "Do not believe every spirit, but test the spirits to see whether they are from God" (1 John 4:1; see also 1 Thessalonians 5:21). That includes testing the people who knock on your door with a smile and a pamphlet. Being polite does not mean being gullible.

Fourth, be kind to the person even when you reject the teaching. Mormon missionaries and Jehovah's Witnesses are often sincere, dedicated people who genuinely believe they are doing God's work. Slamming a door in their face is not how Jesus would respond. You can be firm about the truth and still treat another human being with dignity.

TALKING POINTS

1. Why do you think groups like the Mormons and Jehovah's Witnesses use Christian language and quote the Bible even though their core beliefs are so different from biblical Christianity?

2. The chapter says that Mormonism teaches God was once a human who became God. How does that compare to what the Bible teaches about God in passages like Isaiah 43:10 and John 4:24?

3. The Jehovah's Witnesses changed John 1:1 in their Bible translation. Why would changing a single word in one verse

matter so much? What does it reveal about how they approach Scripture?

4. Both groups are led by centralized human authorities who discourage independent Bible study. Why is that a warning sign? What does the Bible say about testing teachings for yourself?

5. If a Mormon missionary or a Jehovah's Witness knocked on your door this weekend, how would you handle the conversation? What would you want to say, and how would you want to say it?

Frank Abagnale eventually got caught. The truth has a way of surfacing no matter how convincing the disguise. The same principle applies to religious claims. When you know what the real thing looks like, the counterfeits become much easier to spot. You do not need to be an expert on every false teaching in the world. You just need to know the Bible well enough to recognize when someone is handing you something that does not match.

Turn the page.

4

JUDAISM

Have you ever looked through an old family photo album and noticed something surprising? Maybe your grandfather had the same nose you do. Maybe your great-aunt smiled exactly the way your mom smiles. The resemblance is unmistakable. You share the same bloodline, the same family stories, even some of the same habits. But you are also very different people. Your grandfather grew up in a different era, lived in a different place, and saw the world through different eyes. You share roots, but you have grown in different directions.

That is the best way to understand the relationship between Christianity and Judaism. These two faiths are not strangers who happen to live on the same street. They are family. They share the same Scriptures, the same God, the same ancestors, and the same ancient promises. For centuries, they walked the same road together. And then they came to a fork, and the question that divided them was the biggest question in all of human history.

His name was Jesus. And everything depends on what you believe about him.

THE SAME STARTING LINE

Christianity and Judaism both begin with the Old Testament. Christians call it the Old Testament. Jewish people call it the Tanakh, and they organize the books a little differently, but the content is the same. Genesis, Exodus, the Psalms, Isaiah, Daniel. These books belong to both faiths.

That means Jews and Christians share a remarkable amount of common ground. Both believe in one God who created the heavens and the earth. Both believe God chose Abraham and made a covenant with him, promising that through his descendants all the nations of the earth would be blessed (Genesis 12:1–3). Both believe God rescued Israel from slavery in Egypt, gave the Law to Moses on Mount Sinai, and entered into a special relationship with the people of Israel. Both believe the prophets spoke on God's behalf, calling the people to repentance and pointing toward a future hope.

For more than a thousand years, there was no separation at all. The story of the Old Testament is the story of both faiths. Every hero, every villain, every miracle, every failure belongs to Christians and Jews alike. Abraham is the father of both families. Moses led the ancestors of both. David is the king both look back to with pride.

The split did not happen over a minor detail. It happened over the most important promise God ever made.

THE PROMISE OF A MESSIAH

All through the Old Testament, God made promises about someone who was coming. The prophets described a figure who would rescue God's people, establish justice, and reign forever.

This coming figure was called the Messiah, which means "anointed one." It is the same word that gives us the title "Christ."

The prophets painted a vivid picture of what this Messiah would do. He would be born in Bethlehem (Micah 5:2). He would come from the line of David (Isaiah 11:1). He would be a suffering servant who would bear the sins of others (Isaiah 53). He would establish a kingdom that would never end (Daniel 7:13–14).

Both Jews and Christians agree that God made these promises. The disagreement is over whether they have been fulfilled.

THE FORK IN THE ROAD

Christians believe that Jesus of Nazareth was the Messiah. He was born in Bethlehem, descended from David, suffered and died for the sins of the world, and rose from the dead. The promises have been kept. The Messiah has come.

Most Jewish people disagree. And their reasons are worth understanding, because they take the Old Testament just as seriously as Christians do.

Many Jews expected the Messiah to be a political and military leader, someone who would overthrow the enemies of Israel and establish a visible, earthly kingdom. When Jesus showed up as a traveling preacher from a small town, performed miracles, and then allowed himself to be arrested and executed by the Romans, that did not match what many were looking for. A crucified Messiah seemed like a contradiction. How could God's chosen deliverer end up on a Roman cross?

The early Christians answered that question by pointing to passages like Isaiah 53, which describes a servant who is "wounded for our transgressions" and "crushed for our iniquities." They argued that the Messiah was always supposed to suffer first, and that his kingdom was a spiritual one that would transform hearts rather than borders. The resurrection proved that the cross was not a defeat but a victory.

Jewish teachers responded differently. They argued that Isaiah 53 was about the nation of Israel itself, not a single individual. They pointed to messianic passages about peace, justice, and the gathering of all nations, and they said those promises clearly had not been fulfilled yet. The world is still full of war and injustice. If the Messiah had truly come, would things not look different?

This debate has been going on for two thousand years, and it remains the central divide between the two faiths.

THE LAW OF MOSES

Another major difference involves the Law of Moses, the collection of commandments God gave Israel at Mount Sinai. The Torah contains 613 commandments covering everything from worship and sacrifice to diet and clothing. These laws shaped every part of Israelite life and set Israel apart from the surrounding nations.

Judaism teaches that these laws remain binding. Observant Jews still follow dietary laws (called kosher), keep the Sabbath from Friday evening to Saturday evening, and celebrate the biblical festivals such as Passover, Yom Kippur (the Day of Atonement), and Sukkot (the Feast of Tabernacles). The Law is not seen as a burden but as a gift, a blueprint for living in relationship with God.

Christianity sees the Law differently. The New Testament teaches that the Law of Moses served an important purpose, but that purpose has been fulfilled in Christ. Paul wrote that the Law was "our guardian until Christ came, in order that we might be justified by faith" (Galatians 3:24). The Law pointed forward to something greater. Now that Jesus has come, Christians are no longer under the old covenant but under a new one (Hebrews 8:13).

This does not mean the Old Testament is worthless to Christians. Far from it. The moral principles behind the Law still reflect God's character, and the stories of the Old Testament remain essential for understanding God's plan. But the specific regulations about diet, sacrifice, and ceremony were fulfilled in Jesus and are no longer binding on his followers.

This is another area where the fork in the road shows up clearly. Judaism says the Law continues. Christianity says the Law has been completed.

ONE GOD, DIFFERENT UNDERSTANDINGS

Both faiths worship one God, and both take that belief very seriously. The most important prayer in Judaism is the Shema, taken from Deuteronomy 6:4: "Hear, O Israel: The LORD our God, the LORD is one." Jewish people have recited those words morning and evening for thousands of years.

Christians agree that God is one. But as you read in Chapter 1, Christians believe that one God exists in three persons: Father, Son, and Holy Spirit. Jewish teaching firmly rejects this. To most Jewish thinkers, the Trinity looks like a violation of the Shema, an attempt to divide God into parts. They see

Christian worship of Jesus as worship of a human being, which would violate the first commandment.

Christians respond that the Trinity does not divide God. It reveals the fullness of who God has always been. The Old Testament itself contains hints of this: the Spirit of God hovering over the waters in Genesis 1:2, the mysterious "angel of the LORD" who speaks as God in passages like Exodus 3, and the plural language in Genesis 1:26 where God says, "Let *us* make man in *our* image." Christians do not worship three gods. They worship one God who has revealed himself in three persons.

This disagreement runs deep, and it is closely connected to the question about Jesus. If Jesus is not the Messiah, then worshiping him is a serious error. If he is the Messiah and also divine, then refusing to worship him is an equally serious one. There is no comfortable middle ground.

WORSHIP AND DAILY LIFE

Jewish worship centers on the synagogue, which is a place of prayer, study, and community. Services include readings from the Torah (the first five books of the Bible), prayers, and songs. A rabbi serves as a teacher and leader, but the rabbi is not a priest in the way the Old Testament describes. The Temple in Jerusalem, where sacrifices were offered, was destroyed by the Romans in AD 70 and has never been rebuilt. Without a temple, the sacrificial system that was central to Old Testament worship has been on hold for nearly two thousand years.

That detail is worth pausing on. The Old Testament law required animal sacrifices for the forgiveness of sins. The Day of Atonement, described in Leviticus 16, was the most important day of the year, when the high priest entered the Most Holy Place to make atonement for the nation. Without a temple, that system cannot function. Christianity says this is not a problem because Jesus is the final sacrifice, the Lamb of God who takes away the sin of the world (John 1:29). Judaism has had to adapt in other ways, focusing on prayer, repentance, and good deeds as the path to forgiveness.

Jewish daily life is shaped by practices that many Christians would find unfamiliar. Observant Jews follow strict dietary laws, avoiding pork and shellfish and separating meat from dairy. They rest on the Sabbath, refraining from work and many everyday activities from sundown on Friday to sundown on Saturday. They observe annual festivals that retell the great stories of Israel's history, including Passover, which remembers the Exodus from Egypt, and Hanukkah, which celebrates the rededication of the Temple after a period of persecution.

BRANCHES OF JUDAISM

Modern Judaism is not one single movement. There are several major branches, and they differ from each other quite a bit.

Orthodox Judaism is the most traditional branch. Orthodox Jews follow the Torah and the rabbinic traditions closely, keeping kosher, observing the Sabbath strictly, and maintaining traditional practices in worship and daily life. They see the Law as fully binding and unchanging.

Conservative Judaism holds a middle position. Conservative Jews respect tradition but allow for some adaptation to modern life. They still observe the major laws and festivals but are more flexible in how they apply some of the details.

Reform Judaism is the most liberal branch. Reform Jews emphasize the ethical principles of the Torah more than the specific ritual laws. Many Reform Jews do not keep kosher or observe the Sabbath in the traditional way. They see Judaism as an evolving faith that adapts to each generation.

These differences mean that there is no single answer to the question "What do Jews believe?" The range of belief and practice within Judaism is wide. But all branches share a reverence for the Torah, a commitment to the covenant between God and Israel, and a rejection of Jesus as the Messiah.

FAMILY, NOT ENEMIES

Christians owe a deep debt to Judaism. The Bible you hold in your hands was written almost entirely by Jewish authors. Jesus was Jewish. The apostles were Jewish. The early church was made up of Jewish believers who recognized Jesus as the fulfillment of everything their Scriptures had promised. Christianity grew out of Judaism.

That history means Christians should approach Judaism with a respect that goes beyond politeness. This is the soil your faith grew from. Disagreeing about Jesus does not erase the shared roots, and it certainly does not justify the centuries of hostility and persecution that Jewish communities have endured at the hands of people who claimed to follow Christ. That history is a stain on the church, and it is worth acknowledging honestly.

At the same time, respect does not mean avoiding the truth. Christians believe, based on the testimony of the New Testament and the evidence of the resurrection, that Jesus is the

Messiah whom the prophets foretold. That belief is not an insult to Judaism. It is the fulfillment of Judaism's own greatest hope.

WHAT THIS MEANS FOR US

First, shared roots matter. When you talk to a Jewish friend about God, you are not starting from scratch. You share the same Old Testament, the same creation story, the same Ten Commandments, and the same God. That common ground is a gift, not something to skip over.

Second, the Messiah question is *the* question. Every other difference between Christianity and Judaism leads back to this one: Is Jesus the Messiah? If you can explain clearly and kindly why you believe the answer is yes, you have reached the heart of the conversation.

Third, fulfilled does not mean discarded. Christians believe the Law of Moses has been fulfilled in Christ, but that does not mean the Old Testament is unimportant. The Old Testament reveals God's character, tells the story that makes the gospel make sense, and contains promises that point directly to Jesus. Do not neglect it.

Fourth, history carries weight. Jewish people have suffered greatly throughout history, and some of that suffering was inflicted by people who called themselves Christians. Being aware of that history will make you a more compassionate and credible conversation partner.

TALKING POINTS

1. Why do you think the question of whether Jesus is the Messiah became such a deep dividing line between Judaism

and Christianity? Could the two faiths ever resolve that disagreement?

2. Jewish people expected a Messiah who would overthrow Rome and establish an earthly kingdom. Why do you think God's plan looked so different from what people expected?

3. The Temple in Jerusalem was destroyed in AD 70, and animal sacrifices have not been offered since. What does that mean for the Old Testament system of atonement? How do Christians explain this?

4. The chapter mentions that Christianity grew out of Judaism and that Jesus, the apostles, and most early Christians were Jewish. Why is that an important detail to remember?

5. How can you show respect for Judaism and Jewish people while still being honest about your belief that Jesus is the promised Messiah?

Christianity and Judaism share a story that stretches back thousands of years. The fork in the road came when a carpenter from Nazareth stood up and said the wait was over. Whether you follow him or keep waiting, that moment changed the world. And it is that moment, more than any other, that you will want to understand as the conversations ahead get even more complex.

Turn the page.

5

ISLAM

Charles Dickens opened his famous novel *A Tale of Two Cities* by piling contrast on top of contrast. "It was the best of times, it was the worst of times, it was the age of wisdom, it was the age of foolishness." The story is set in two great cities, London and Paris, during the years surrounding the French Revolution. The two cities are connected by history and by the lives of the characters who move between them. But they are heading in very different directions. What looks like a shared story on the surface turns out to be two very different stories underneath.

Dickens could have been describing Christianity and Islam. These two faiths are connected by history, by shared figures like Abraham and Jesus, and by the conviction that there is one God who created the world. They are the two largest religions on the planet, and from a distance they can seem like neighbors living on the same street. But the closer you look, the more you realize that the shared vocabulary hides deep disagreements. The God they describe, the Jesus they honor, and the salvation they offer are not the same. Like London and

Paris in Dickens' novel, Christianity and Islam share a story but are heading in very different directions.

HOW ISLAM BEGAN

Islam was founded in the seventh century AD by a man named Muhammad, born around AD 570 in the city of Mecca in what is now Saudi Arabia. Mecca was a busy trading center and a religious hub where Arabs worshiped many different gods. Muhammad grew up in this environment but became dissatisfied with the idol worship around him.

When he was about forty years old, Muhammad reported that the angel Gabriel appeared to him in a cave and began delivering messages from God. These messages continued for the next twenty-three years and were eventually collected into a book called the Quran, which Muslims regard as the final and perfect word of God. Muslims believe the Quran was not written by Muhammad but was dictated directly by God through Gabriel, word for word.

Muhammad began preaching in Mecca, calling people to abandon their idols and submit to the one true God. The word "Islam" itself means "submission," and a "Muslim" is "one who submits." His message was not popular at first. He faced opposition, threats, and eventually fled to the city of Medina in AD 622. That migration, called the Hijra, marks the beginning of the Islamic calendar. Over the next decade, Muhammad gathered followers, built an army, and returned to conquer Mecca. By the time he died in AD 632, Islam had spread across much of the Arabian Peninsula.

THE QURAN

The Quran is the central text of Islam. It is roughly the length of the New Testament and is divided into 114 chapters called surahs. Muslims believe it is the literal word of God, unchanged and unchangeable. It is recited in Arabic, and many Muslims believe the Quran can only be fully understood in its original language.

The Quran contains stories that will sound familiar to anyone who has read the Bible. Adam, Noah, Abraham, Moses, David, and Jesus all appear. But the versions of these stories often differ from the biblical accounts in important ways. For example, the Quran teaches that Abraham was commanded to sacrifice Ishmael, not Isaac (though the Quran does not name the son directly, Islamic tradition identifies him as Ishmael). That difference matters because the Bible specifically names Isaac (Genesis 22:2), and the entire biblical story of God's covenant people flows through Isaac, not Ishmael.

Muslims also accept earlier writings called the Hadith, which are collections of sayings and actions attributed to Muhammad. The Hadith are not considered equal to the Quran, but they carry significant authority and shape how Muslims understand and apply their faith in daily life.

THE FIVE PILLARS

Islam is built around five core practices known as the Five Pillars. These are the framework of a faithful Muslim's life.

The first pillar is the Shahada, the declaration of faith: "There is no god but God, and Muhammad is the messenger of God." Reciting this statement with sincerity is what makes a person a Muslim.

The second pillar is Salat, the practice of praying five times a day while facing the city of Mecca. These prayers follow a specific pattern of words, postures, and movements. They happen at dawn, midday, mid-afternoon, sunset, and evening, and they structure the entire day around submission to God.

The third pillar is Zakat, giving a portion of one's wealth to those in need. This is not optional charity. It is an obligation, typically set at 2.5% of a person's savings each year.

The fourth pillar is Sawm, fasting during the month of Ramadan. From sunrise to sunset each day during Ramadan, Muslims abstain from food, drink, and other physical needs. The fast is meant to develop self-discipline and draw the believer closer to God.

The fifth pillar is the Hajj, a pilgrimage to Mecca that every Muslim is expected to make at least once in their lifetime if they are physically and financially able. Millions of Muslims make this journey each year, and it is considered one of the most important acts of devotion in the Islamic faith.

These pillars give Islam a structured, disciplined character. But notice what is missing from the list. There is no mention of grace, no mention of a savior, and no mention of a sacrifice for sin. The emphasis is entirely on what the believer does for God, not on what God has done for the believer.

ONE GOD, BUT NOT THE SAME GOD

Islam insists on the absolute oneness of God, a principle called tawhid. Muslims worship Allah, and they say firmly that God is one and has no partners, no son, and no equal. The Quran states, "He neither begets nor is born" (Surah 112:3), a verse that directly contradicts the Christian belief that Jesus is the Son of God.

This is the sharpest theological divide between Christianity and Islam. Christians believe in the Trinity: one God in three persons. Muslims consider the Trinity a form of polytheism, a grave sin in Islam called shirk. Shirk, associating anything or anyone with God, is described in the Quran as the one unforgivable sin.

Some people try to smooth this over by saying that Christians and Muslims worship the same God and just describe him differently. But the differences are not minor adjustments. The God of Christianity is a Father who sent his Son to die for sinners and who sent his Spirit to dwell in believers. The God of Islam has no son, requires no sacrifice, and relates to humanity primarily as a master relates to servants. These are not two descriptions of the same person. They are descriptions of two fundamentally different beings.

ISLAM'S JESUS

Jesus holds a unique place in Islam. The Quran mentions him by name (using the Arabic form Isa) more than two dozen times. Muslims honor Jesus as a great prophet, one of the most important messengers God ever sent. They affirm that he was born of a virgin, that he performed miracles, and that he lived a sinless life.

But that is where the agreement ends.

Islam denies that Jesus is the Son of God. It denies that he is divine. And most significantly, it denies that he was crucified. The Quran says, "They did not kill him, nor did they crucify him; but another was made to resemble him to them" (Surah 4:157). According to Islamic teaching, God rescued Jesus from the cross and raised him to heaven, and someone else died in his place.

This is a direct contradiction of the most well-documented event in the New Testament. The crucifixion of Jesus is confirmed not only by all four Gospels but also by non-Christian historians of the first century. More importantly, if Jesus was not crucified, then there was no sacrifice for sin. And if there was no sacrifice for sin, the entire gospel falls apart. Christianity without the cross is not Christianity at all.

Islam replaces the crucifixion with the idea that Jesus was simply a prophet who delivered God's message and was then taken up to heaven. He is honored, but he is not worshiped. He is respected, but he is not the Savior. The Jesus of Islam and the Jesus of the Bible share a name, but they play very different roles in very different stories.

SALVATION IN ISLAM

In Christianity, salvation is a gift of grace received through faith and obedience to the gospel. In Islam, salvation works differently. There is no need for a savior to pay the penalty for human rebellion. Instead, each person is judged individually by their deeds. On the Day of Judgment, Allah will weigh every person's good and bad actions on a scale. If the good outweighs the bad, the person enters paradise. If not, they face punishment.

There is one important exception. Allah is described as merciful, and he may choose to forgive whomever he wishes.

But there is no guarantee. Even Muhammad himself, according to the Hadith, expressed uncertainty about his own eternal fate. Muslims hope for God's mercy, but they cannot be sure of it.

Compare that to the confidence the New Testament offers. "There is therefore now no condemnation for those who are in Christ Jesus" (Romans 8:1). Christianity does not leave salvation up to a scale. It places it in the hands of a Savior who has already done what no human being could do for themselves.

SUNNI AND SHIA

Shortly after Muhammad's death, a dispute arose over who should lead the Muslim community. One group believed leadership should pass to Muhammad's close companion Abu Bakr. Another group insisted it should go to Ali, Muhammad's cousin and son-in-law. This disagreement created a split that has persisted for nearly 1,400 years.

The larger group became known as Sunni Muslims, and they make up roughly 85–90% of the world's Muslim population. The smaller group became known as Shia Muslims, concentrated primarily in Iran, Iraq, and parts of Lebanon. While both groups share the core beliefs of Islam, they differ on matters of leadership, religious authority, and certain practices. The division has fueled political conflicts and sectarian violence throughout history and continues to shape the Muslim world today.

ISLAM AND THE WORLD

Islam is the second-largest religion in the world, with nearly two billion followers. It spans continents and cultures, from the Middle East to Southeast Asia to Africa to Europe and the Americas. Its influence on art, architecture, science, and law throughout history has been enormous, and its impact on global events today is impossible to ignore.

For Christians, understanding Islam is not just an academic exercise. Muslims are your neighbors, classmates, and coworkers. Many of them are deeply devoted to God and live lives of impressive discipline and generosity. Treating them with respect and dignity is not optional. It is what Jesus commands.

But respect does not require agreement, and kindness does not require silence. When the Quran contradicts the Bible, both cannot be right. When Islam says Jesus was not crucified and Christianity says the cross is the center of everything, someone is wrong. The question is not whether the disagreement is uncomfortable. The question is where the evidence leads.

WHAT THIS MEANS FOR US

First, similarities can be misleading. Islam and Christianity share enough vocabulary and history to seem compatible at first glance. Do not let surface-level similarities keep you from examining the deeper differences. The most important questions—who is Jesus and how are people saved—receive very different answers.

Second, the cross is the dividing line. Islam honors Jesus but removes the cross. Christianity puts the cross at the center of everything. If you understand why the cross matters, you understand the most important difference between these two faiths.

Third, works versus grace is a theme you will see again. Islam is built on a system of earned merit, where your deeds determine your destiny. Christianity is built on grace, where your destiny is determined by what Jesus has already done. Keep this contrast in mind as you encounter other religions in the chapters ahead.

Fourth, know your Muslim neighbor. With nearly two billion Muslims in the world, the chances are good that you will interact with Muslim people throughout your life. Learn what they actually believe rather than relying on stereotypes. And let your conversations be marked by both truth and kindness.

TALKING POINTS

1. Islam teaches that Jesus was a great prophet but not the Son of God and was not crucified. Why is the crucifixion so important to Christianity that removing it changes everything?
2. The Five Pillars of Islam are all things the believer does for God. How does that compare to the Christian gospel, where the emphasis is on what God has done for the believer?
3. The Quran tells many of the same stories as the Bible but changes key details, like which son Abraham was asked to sacrifice. Why do those details matter? How would you decide which version to trust?
4. Islam teaches that on Judgment Day, God will weigh a person's good deeds against their bad deeds. What problems do you see with that system? How does the Christian view of judgment differ?
5. How can you have an honest conversation about faith with a Muslim friend without being disrespectful? What attitudes and habits would help that conversation go well?

Christianity and Islam are the two largest religions on the planet, and they are growing side by side in communities all over the world. Like Dickens' two cities, they share a story but are heading in different directions. The conversation between them is not going away. It is getting louder. The better you understand what Islam teaches and why it differs from the gospel, the more prepared you will be to engage that conversation with both confidence and compassion. You do not need to be afraid of the questions. You just need to be rooted deeply enough in the truth to answer them.

Turn the page.

6

HINDUISM

The comedy *Groundhog Day* stars Bill Murray as Phil Connors, an arrogant TV weatherman who travels to the small town of Punxsutawney, Pennsylvania, to cover the annual Groundhog Day celebration. He hates the assignment, insults the locals, and cannot wait to leave. But the next morning, Phil wakes up and discovers that it is Groundhog Day again. The same song plays on the alarm clock. The same people say the same things. The same events unfold in the same order. No matter what Phil does, he wakes up the next morning to the same day, over and over and over.

At first, Phil panics. Then he takes advantage of the loop, using his knowledge of each repeated day to manipulate people and get what he wants. But nothing satisfies him. Eventually, Phil begins to change. He learns to play piano. He helps strangers. He becomes genuinely kind. And only when he has transformed into a truly good person does the cycle finally break. He wakes up on February 3rd, a new man living a new day.

That movie is a surprisingly good introduction to Hinduism. Not because Hindus watch *Groundhog Day* in their temples, but because the story captures something central to the Hindu worldview: life is a cycle, and the way you live determines whether you stay trapped in it or finally break free. Hinduism teaches that every soul is caught in a loop of birth, death, and rebirth, and that the goal of life is to escape that loop once and for all.

A RELIGION WITHOUT A FOUNDER

Every religion you have studied so far can be traced to a specific origin. Christianity begins with Jesus. Islam begins with Muhammad. Mormonism begins with Joseph Smith. Hinduism is different. It has no single founder, no single moment of origin, and no single book that defines it. Instead, Hinduism developed gradually over thousands of years in the Indian subcontinent, absorbing ideas, stories, and practices from many different cultures and traditions along the way.

The roots of Hinduism stretch back at least 4,000 years, making it one of the oldest living religious traditions on the planet. Because it grew over such a long period rather than being launched by one person, Hinduism is extraordinarily diverse. It contains so many beliefs, practices, gods, and philosophies that some scholars describe it less as a single religion and more as a family of related traditions that share certain core ideas.

That diversity can make Hinduism hard to summarize. But there are several key beliefs that most Hindus hold in common, and those beliefs paint a very different picture of reality than the one you find in the Bible.

BRAHMAN AND THE GODS

At the deepest level, Hinduism teaches that there is one ultimate reality called Brahman. Brahman is not a person. It is not a being you can talk to or have a relationship with. It is more like an infinite, impersonal force or energy that underlies everything in the universe. Everything that exists is, in some sense, a part of Brahman or an expression of Brahman.

If that sounds abstract, it is. And that is partly why Hinduism also has gods. Lots of them. Hindu tradition speaks of millions of deities, though the most prominent are Brahma (the creator), Vishnu (the preserver), and Shiva (the destroyer). Each of these gods takes many forms. Vishnu alone is said to have appeared on earth in ten different avatars, or incarnations, including Rama and Krishna, two of the most beloved figures in Hindu devotion.

Some Hindus focus their worship on one particular god and treat that god as supreme. Others worship many gods depending on the occasion or need. Still others see all the gods as different faces of the one Brahman, the way light passing through a prism splits into many colors but remains one light.

This is a world away from the Bible's teaching. The God of Christianity is not an impersonal force. He is a personal being who speaks, loves, acts, and enters into relationship with his creation. And the Bible is emphatic that there is only one God. "I am the LORD, and there is no other, besides me there is no God" (Isaiah 45:5). The gods of Hinduism, whether understood as real beings or as symbols of a deeper reality, represent a fundamentally different answer to the question of who or what is at the center of the universe.

SACRED TEXTS

Hinduism has a vast library of sacred writings, far larger than the Bible. The oldest and most authoritative are the Vedas, a collection of hymns, prayers, and rituals composed over a thousand years. The Upanishads, written later, explore deeper philosophical questions about the nature of Brahman, the soul, and reality.

The most widely known Hindu text is probably the Bhagavad Gita, a section of a much longer epic called the Mahabharata. The Gita is a conversation between a warrior prince named Arjuna and the god Krishna, who serves as his chariot driver. On the eve of a great battle, Arjuna is paralyzed by doubt about whether it is right to fight. Krishna responds with a long teaching about duty, devotion, and the nature of the soul. The Gita is cherished by Hindus and is often compared in importance to how Christians view the Gospels.

Another major epic is the Ramayana, which tells the story of Prince Rama and his quest to rescue his wife Sita from a demon king. These stories are deeply woven into Hindu culture and are retold through festivals, art, dance, and film across India and beyond.

Unlike the Bible, which Christians treat as the single, sufficient authority for faith, Hinduism does not depend on one text or even one set of texts. Its scriptures are vast, varied, and open to many interpretations. There is no Hindu equivalent of "the Bible says," because there is no single book that functions as the final word.

KARMA

One of the most well-known Hindu concepts is karma. You have probably heard the word before, maybe in a casual way, like someone saying "that's bad karma" after a friend does something selfish. But in Hinduism, karma is much more serious than a figure of speech.

Karma is the law of moral cause and effect. Every action you take, whether good or bad, produces a result that will come back to you. Good actions produce good results. Bad actions produce bad results. And these results do not expire at death. They carry over from one life to the next.

Think of it like a bank account that never closes. Every kind word, every generous act, every honest choice adds to the balance. Every lie, every act of cruelty, every selfish decision subtracts from it. When you die, the balance you have built up determines what kind of life you are born into next. A life well lived might lead to rebirth in a higher position. A life lived badly might lead to rebirth in a lower one, even as an animal or an insect.

Karma creates a system where you are entirely responsible for your own fate. There is no grace in the Hindu understanding of karma. There is no savior who steps in to pay a debt you cannot pay. What you get is what you have earned, across as many lifetimes as it takes.

The Bible sees the human situation very differently. Yes, actions have consequences. But the deepest problem is not a bad balance in a cosmic ledger. The deepest problem is a broken relationship with God, and no amount of good behavior can fix it on its own. That is why Christianity offers grace: "For by grace you have been saved through faith. And this is not your own doing; it is the gift of God, not a result of works, so that no one may boast" (Ephesians 2:8–9).

REINCARNATION AND SAMSARA

Karma powers a cycle that Hindus call samsara, the endless wheel of birth, death, and rebirth. When a person dies, the soul does not go to heaven or hell. It is reborn into a new body, and the kind of body it receives depends on the karma accumulated in previous lives. This cycle repeats over and over, potentially for millions of lifetimes.

Samsara is not something Hindus look forward to. It is something they want to escape. Being reborn again and again is seen as a kind of trap, a weary repetition of suffering and struggle. The goal is not to keep cycling through better and better lives. The goal is to get off the wheel entirely.

Christianity has a completely different view of life and death. The Bible teaches that "it is appointed for man to die once, and after that comes judgment" (Hebrews 9:27). There is no second chance, no do-over, no next life to try again. You live once, you die once, and then you stand before God. That might sound harsher than reincarnation, but it actually gives each life an urgency and a dignity that the cycle of samsara does not. Every moment matters because you do not get a million more tries. This life, right now, is the one that counts.

And the Christian hope after death is not another spin on the wheel. It is resurrection, a new body and a new creation where sin and death are gone for good.

MOKSHA: BREAKING FREE

The ultimate goal in Hinduism is moksha, which means liberation or release. Moksha is the moment when the soul escapes the cycle of samsara and is united with Brahman, the way a drop of water is absorbed back into the ocean. Individual identity fades. The soul is no longer a separate self. It merges into the infinite.

Hindu tradition describes several paths to moksha. The path of knowledge involves deep meditation and philosophical study, coming to understand that your true self and Brahman are one and the same. The path of devotion involves wholehearted worship of a particular god, surrendering yourself completely to that deity. The path of action involves performing your duties selflessly, without attachment to the results.

These paths are not mutually exclusive. Many Hindus practice a combination of all three. But the destination is the same: escape from the cycle and absorption into the ultimate.

For a Christian, this raises an important question. Is the goal of existence to lose yourself, or to be found? Christianity does not teach that you will be absorbed into God like a drop of water disappearing into the sea. It teaches that God made you as an individual, loves you as an individual, and will raise you as an individual to live with him forever. Your identity is not an illusion to be shed. It is a gift to be redeemed.

THE CASTE SYSTEM

One of the most controversial aspects of Hinduism is the caste system, a social structure that has shaped Indian society for thousands of years. Traditionally, Hindu society was divided into four main groups, or varnas: the Brahmins (priests and teachers), the Kshatriyas (warriors and rulers), the Vaishyas (merchants and farmers), and the Shudras (laborers and servants). Below these four groups were people considered outside the system entirely, historically called "untouchables."

A person's caste was determined by birth, and for most of Indian history, moving between castes was nearly impossible. The system was deeply tied to karma. If you were born into a low caste, it was understood as the result of bad karma from a previous life. If you fulfilled your duties faithfully, you might be reborn into a higher caste next time.

Modern India has officially outlawed caste-based discrimination, and many Hindus today reject the rigid caste system. But its influence on culture and society is far from gone, and it remains a sensitive and complicated issue.

The Bible offers a starkly different vision. "There is neither Jew nor Greek, there is neither slave nor free, there is no male and female, for you are all one in Christ Jesus" (Galatians 3:28). The gospel does not sort people into ranks based on their birth. It declares that every person, regardless of background, is made in the image of God and is equally loved by him. That is a message the world still desperately needs.

WHAT THIS MEANS FOR US

First, the personal matters. Hinduism's ultimate reality, Brahman, is impersonal. You cannot know Brahman the way you know a friend or a parent. The God of the Bible is different. He knows your name, hears your prayers, and invites you into relationship. Never take that for granted.

Second, grace breaks the cycle. Karma says you get what you deserve, forever. The gospel says God gives you what you do not deserve: forgiveness, mercy, and a fresh start. That is the difference between a religion of earning and a faith built on a gift.

Third, one life means one life matters. Reincarnation spreads meaning across millions of lives. The Bible concentrates it into one. That makes every choice, every relationship, and every day more significant, not less.

Fourth, every person has equal worth. Any system that ranks human beings by birth, whether it is an ancient caste system or a modern prejudice, contradicts the Bible's teaching that all people are created in God's image. Let that truth shape the way you treat everyone you meet.

TALKING POINTS

1. Hinduism has millions of gods, while Christianity insists there is only one. Why does it matter whether there is one God or many? How does it change the way you think about worship, truth, and morality?

2. Karma says you earn your fate through your actions across many lives. Grace says God gives you what you could never earn. Which view of justice makes more sense to you, and why?

3. Hinduism teaches that the goal of life is to escape the cycle of rebirth and merge with Brahman. Christianity teaches that the goal is resurrection and eternal life with God as an individual. What difference does it make whether you lose your identity or keep it?

4. The caste system ranked people by birth and connected social status to karma from past lives. How does the Bible's teaching that all people are made in God's image challenge that kind of thinking?

5. Hinduism is one of the oldest major religions in the world, and its age is sometimes used as an argument for its truth. Do you think the age of a belief system makes it more likely to be true? Why or why not?

Phil Connors spent what felt like an eternity trapped in the same day before he finally broke free. Hinduism offers its own version of that story, a soul cycling through lifetime after lifetime, trying to earn its way out of the loop. Christianity tells a different story. You do not have to earn your way out of anything. Someone has already broken the cycle for you. The question is not whether you can accumulate enough good karma across a thousand lifetimes. The question is whether you will trust the One who offers to set you free right now, in this life, the only one you have.

Turn the page.

7

BUDDHISM

Think about something you wanted badly. Maybe it was a video game you had been asking for since your birthday. Maybe it was making the starting lineup on your team. Maybe it was a pair of shoes you saw every time you walked through the mall. You thought about it constantly. You pictured how great it would feel when you finally got it. And then, one day, you did.

It felt amazing. For about a week.

Then the game got repetitive. The season was harder than you expected. The shoes got scuffed. The excitement faded, and you found yourself looking at the next thing, the next want, the next "if I could just have *that*, I would be happy." The cycle started all over again.

You have just experienced, in miniature, the core insight of Buddhism. Twenty-five hundred years ago, a man in India looked at that cycle and decided it was the root of all human suffering. He did not turn to God for a solution. He did not pray for help. He sat down under a tree and tried to think his way out. And what he came up with became one of the largest and most influential religions in the history of the world.

His name was Siddhartha Gautama, and the world would come to know him as the Buddha.

THE PRINCE WHO LEFT EVERYTHING

Siddhartha Gautama was born around 563 BC in what is now Nepal, into a wealthy royal family. According to tradition, his father was a king who wanted to protect his son from the harsh realities of life. Siddhartha grew up surrounded by luxury, shielded from sickness, old age, and death. He had everything a young man could want: comfort, wealth, a wife, and a son.

But the walls could not hold forever. The story says that on a series of trips outside the palace, Siddhartha encountered four sights that shattered his sheltered world: a frail old man, a person ravaged by disease, a dead body being carried to a funeral, and a wandering monk who had given up all possessions in search of peace. These encounters stunned Siddhartha. For the first time, he realized that suffering was unavoidable. No amount of wealth or pleasure could protect anyone from aging, sickness, and death.

At the age of twenty-nine, Siddhartha made a radical decision. He abandoned his palace, his family, and his inheritance. He shaved his head, put on simple robes, and set out to find the answer to one question: How can suffering be overcome?

He spent years trying different approaches. He studied under religious teachers. He practiced extreme fasting and self-denial until his body was nearly destroyed. Nothing worked. Finally, he sat down beneath a fig tree (later called the Bodhi tree) and resolved not to move until he had found the answer. After a long night of deep meditation, he believed he had achieved enlightenment. From that point on, he was known as the Buddha, a title meaning "the awakened one."

THE FOUR NOBLE TRUTHS

The Buddha's core teaching is organized around four statements known as the Four Noble Truths. These are the foundation of everything in Buddhism.

The First Noble Truth is that life is suffering. The word the Buddha used was dukkha, which covers everything from obvious pain like illness and grief to the subtle dissatisfaction that runs underneath even the good moments. That restless feeling you get after the excitement of a new purchase wears off? That is dukkha. Buddhism says it is woven into the fabric of existence itself.

The Second Noble Truth is that suffering is caused by desire and attachment. We suffer because we cling to things that cannot last. We want pleasure, possessions, status, and security, and we are devastated when they slip away. Even our attachment to people we love becomes a source of pain because nothing in this world is permanent.

The Third Noble Truth is that suffering can end. If desire is the cause, then eliminating desire is the cure. The Buddha taught that it is possible to reach a state where craving and attachment no longer control you, and when that happens, suffering dissolves.

The Fourth Noble Truth is the path that leads to the end of suffering. The Buddha called it the Eightfold Path, and it is essentially a program for training your mind, your speech, and your behavior so that desire loses its grip on you.

THE EIGHTFOLD PATH

The Eightfold Path is Buddhism's practical guide for how to live. It is divided into three categories: wisdom, ethical conduct, and mental discipline.

Under wisdom, the path calls for right understanding (seeing reality as it truly is) and right intention (committing to the path of compassion and letting go of harmful desires).

Under ethical conduct, it calls for right speech (avoiding lies, gossip, and harsh words), right action (not harming living beings, not stealing, not acting selfishly), and right livelihood (earning a living in a way that does not cause harm to others).

Under mental discipline, it calls for right effort (cultivating positive states of mind), right mindfulness (being fully aware of your thoughts, feelings, and surroundings in each moment), and right concentration (developing deep focus through meditation).

If this sounds more like a self-improvement program than a religion, that is because in many ways it is. The Eightfold Path is not about pleasing a god. It is about training yourself. The Buddha did not claim to be divine. He did not claim to speak for God. He claimed to have discovered a truth about the nature of suffering and offered a method for dealing with it. The work, from start to finish, is on you.

A RELIGION WITHOUT A GOD

Here is what makes Buddhism truly unique among the world's major religions: it does not require belief in God. The Buddha did not deny that gods might exist. He simply treated the question as irrelevant. Whether or not there is a God, he taught, you still suffer. Whether or not there is a God, you still need to deal with desire and attachment. The solution the Buddha offered does not depend on any being outside yourself. It depends entirely on your own effort, your own discipline, and your own mind.

This is a staggering departure from everything you have read in this book so far. Christianity, Judaism, and Islam all begin with God. Hinduism begins with Brahman. Buddhism begins with you. There is no creator to worship, no savior to trust, no prayer to offer, and no revelation to obey. You are your own project.

From a Christian perspective, this is both Buddhism's most honest feature and its most devastating weakness. Buddhism is honest because it takes suffering seriously. The Bible agrees that the world is broken and full of pain. "The whole creation has been groaning together in the pains of childbirth until now" (Romans 8:22). But Christianity says the brokenness is not just something to manage or think your way past. It is the result of sin, and the solution requires someone bigger than you.

The idea that a human being can solve the deepest problem of existence through willpower and meditation alone is an enormous claim. Christianity says you cannot save yourself, and that the evidence for this is all around you. If people could fix themselves, they would have done it by now.

NIRVANA

The ultimate goal in Buddhism is nirvana. The word literally means "blowing out," like a candle flame being extinguished.

Nirvana is the state in which desire, hatred, and ignorance have been completely eliminated. When a person reaches nirvana, they are freed from the cycle of death and rebirth. The suffering ends. The wheel stops turning.

But what exactly nirvana *is* remains deliberately vague. The Buddha resisted describing it in concrete terms. It is not heaven. It is not a place. It is not an eternal life with God. It is more like the absence of everything that causes pain, a perfect stillness where the self, as you know it, ceases to be a problem.

Compare that to the Christian hope. The Bible does not offer an escape into blankness. It offers resurrection: a real body, a real world made new, and a real relationship with a God who knows you and loves you. "He will wipe away every tear from their eyes, and death shall be no more" (Revelation 21:4). The Christian future is not the blowing out of a flame. It is the lighting of one that will never go out.

KARMA AND REBIRTH

Like Hinduism, Buddhism teaches karma and rebirth. Your actions in this life affect what happens in the next. But there is an important difference. Hinduism teaches that an eternal soul moves from body to body across lifetimes. Buddhism denies the existence of a permanent soul altogether. What gets reborn is not "you" in any lasting sense but a stream of energy and consciousness shaped by your karma. One common illustration is a candle flame being passed from one candle to another: the flame continues, but it is not the same flame.

This teaching makes rebirth in Buddhism even more puzzling than in Hinduism. If there is no "you" that carries over, then who exactly is being liberated? Buddhism's answer is that this question itself is part of the illusion. The belief in a permanent self is one of the attachments you need to release.

Christianity takes the opposite approach. You are a real person with a real soul, created by a real God. Your identity is not an illusion. Jesus did not die for a stream of consciousness. He died for you.

BRANCHES OF BUDDHISM

Over the centuries, Buddhism has split into several major branches, each with its own emphasis and style.

Theravada Buddhism is the oldest surviving branch and is most common in Sri Lanka, Thailand, Myanmar, and other parts of Southeast Asia. It focuses closely on the original teachings of the Buddha and emphasizes monastic life. Monks in Theravada Buddhism follow strict rules of discipline, live simply, and devote themselves to meditation and study. The path to enlightenment in this tradition is seen as a long, demanding process that may take many lifetimes.

Mahayana Buddhism is the largest branch and is found throughout China, Japan, Korea, and Vietnam. Mahayana introduced the idea of bodhisattvas, enlightened beings who delay their own entry into nirvana in order to help others along the path. This branch is generally more open to the idea that ordinary people, not just monks, can make progress toward enlightenment. It also developed more elaborate rituals, art, and devotional practices.

Zen Buddhism, which grew out of Mahayana in China and Japan, emphasizes meditation above all else. Zen is known for its stripped-down simplicity: quiet sitting, puzzling riddles called koans, and the pursuit of sudden insight. It has become popular in the West, often detached from its religious roots and marketed as a tool for stress relief and mindfulness.

Each branch looks and feels different, but all share the core conviction that suffering is the problem, desire is the cause, and disciplined effort is the way out.

BUDDHISM AND THE BIG QUESTIONS

Buddhism asks some of the right questions. Why do we suffer? Why does getting what we want never fully satisfy us? How should we live in a world full of pain? These are real questions, and the Buddha's honesty about them is one reason his teachings have endured for two and a half thousand years.

But the answers Buddhism offers leave some important gaps. If there is no God, then there is no ultimate standard of right and wrong beyond human opinion. If there is no soul, then human dignity becomes a harder case to make. If the best hope is nirvana, an extinguishing of desire rather than a fulfillment of it, then the deepest longings of the human heart are treated as enemies to be destroyed rather than signals pointing to something real.

Christianity says your desire for love, purpose, and meaning is not the problem. The problem is looking for those things in the wrong places. God made you with a hunger that only he can fill. The restlessness you feel is not proof that desire is bad. It is proof that you were made for something this world cannot provide. As the early church writer Augustine once put it, our hearts are restless until they find their rest in God.

WHAT THIS MEANS FOR US

First, take suffering seriously. Buddhism's willingness to confront suffering head-on is something Christians should respect. Do not dismiss the question. The Bible takes suffering seriously too. The difference is in the answer: Christianity says suffering is real, but it is not the last word. Resurrection is.

Second, desire is not the enemy. Buddhism says eliminate desire. Christianity says redirect it. God gave you the capacity to want, to love, to long for something greater. The goal is not to stop wanting. The goal is to want the right things.

Third, you cannot save yourself. The Eightfold Path puts the entire burden on the individual. Christianity says the honest truth is that you need help. Recognizing your need for a savior is not weakness. It is wisdom.

Fourth, mindfulness is not the same as prayer. Buddhist meditation empties the mind. Christian prayer fills it with conversation with a God who hears and responds. Being still and reflective is good, but it matters enormously whether you are listening to silence or listening for a voice.

TALKING POINTS

1. Buddhism says desire is the root of all suffering. Do you agree? Can you think of examples where desire leads to something good instead of something painful?
2. The Eightfold Path is entirely about self-improvement through personal effort. What is appealing about that idea? What are its limits?

3. Buddhism does not require belief in God. Why do you think a religion without God appeals to so many people? What does it reveal about what people are looking for?

4. The chapter contrasts nirvana (the blowing out of a flame) with the Christian hope of resurrection (a flame that never goes out). Which vision of the future makes more sense to you, and why?

5. Buddhism has become popular in Western culture, often in the form of mindfulness and meditation apps. What is the difference between using Buddhist techniques for relaxation and actually following Buddhism as a religion? Does the distinction matter?

The Buddha looked at the same broken world that the Bible describes, and he was not wrong that something needed to change. Where he went wrong was in the direction he turned. He turned inward, convinced that the answer was inside the human mind. Christianity turns upward, convinced that the answer is found in a God who entered the broken world himself. Both paths take suffering seriously. Only one offers a Savior who suffered with you and for you, and who promises that suffering will not have the final word.

Turn the page.

8

CHINESE TRADITIONAL AND FOLK RELIGIONS

Lewis Carroll's *Alice's Adventures in Wonderland* drops its heroine into a world where nothing follows a single set of rules. Alice meets a caterpillar who speaks in riddles on top of a mushroom. She attends a tea party where time has stopped and the Mad Hatter operates by his own bizarre logic. She plays croquet with the Queen of Hearts, who changes the rules whenever she feels like it and screams "Off with their heads!" at anyone who objects. Every corner of Wonderland has its own personality, its own customs, and its own way of making sense of things. None of them agree with each other. But somehow, they all coexist in the same strange world.

Wonderland is fiction, of course. But if you want to understand Chinese traditional religion, Carroll's mixed-up world is not a bad place to start. For centuries, the religious life of China has not been organized around a single faith the way Christianity, Islam, or Judaism centers on one set of beliefs. Instead, it blends several traditions together, drawing freely from Confucianism, Taoism, and Buddhism without treating them as competitors. A person might follow Confucian ethics at work, visit a Taoist temple for guidance, honor Buddhist monks at a funeral, and pay respects to their ancestors at a family shrine, all in the same week, without seeing any contradiction.

To Western eyes, this looks confusing. How can you follow three religions at once? But in the Chinese tradition, religion is less about choosing the right set of beliefs and more about maintaining harmony, balance, and proper relationships. The question is not "which system is true?" The question is "what practice fits this moment?"

That approach to religion is very different from what you have learned so far in this book. And it raises some important questions.

THREE STREAMS, ONE RIVER

Chinese traditional religion is often described as three streams flowing into one river. The three streams are Confucianism, Taoism, and Buddhism. Each one contributes something different. Confucianism provides ethics and social order. Taoism provides a philosophy of nature and balance. Buddhism, which arrived in China from India roughly two thousand years ago, provides teachings about suffering, karma, and the afterlife. Layered on top of all three is a deep tradition of ancestor veneration and folk practices involving spirits, temples, and festivals.

Most Chinese people who practice these traditions do not sit down and sort them into separate categories. They simply live in a culture where all three are present, the way you might live in a house where different rooms serve different purposes without feeling the need to choose only one room to spend your life in.

To understand the blend, you need to understand each ingredient.

CONFUCIANISM: THE WAY OF ORDER

Confucius was born around 551 BC in the state of Lu, in what is now eastern China. He lived during a time of political chaos, when rival kingdoms fought constantly and social order was breaking down. Confucius believed the solution was not new laws or new armies but a return to proper relationships and moral behavior.

Confucianism is not a religion in the way most Westerners think of religion. Confucius did not talk much about God, the afterlife, or the supernatural. When asked about spiritual matters, he famously said, "If you cannot serve men, how can you serve spirits? If you do not understand life, how can you understand death?" His focus was squarely on this world: how people should treat each other, how families should function, and how societies should be governed.

At the heart of Confucian teaching are five key relationships: ruler and subject, parent and child, husband and wife, older sibling and younger sibling, and friend and friend. Each relationship carries specific duties. The superior is expected to be benevolent and just. The subordinate is expected to be loyal and respectful. When everyone fulfills their role, harmony results. When they do not, chaos follows.

The most important of these relationships is the bond between parent and child. Confucianism places enormous weight on filial piety, the duty of children to honor, respect, and care for their parents. This value extends beyond death. Honoring your ancestors is not just a cultural tradition in China. It is a moral obligation rooted in Confucian teaching.

Confucius also emphasized the importance of education, self-improvement, and ritual. He taught that a truly good person, what he called a "gentleman" or "superior person," cultivates virtue through study, discipline, and practice. His teachings were collected by his students in a book called the Analects, which remains one of the most influential texts in Chinese history.

There is much to admire in Confucian ethics. Respect for parents, honesty, kindness, and social responsibility are values the Bible also upholds. But Confucianism has a significant blind spot. It offers a moral code without a moral foundation. If there is no God who defines right and wrong, then the entire system rests on human tradition and human opinion. Confucius was a wise man, but wisdom that begins and ends with human effort has no anchor outside itself.

TAOISM: THE WAY OF NATURE

Taoism (sometimes spelled Daoism) traces its roots to a figure named Lao Tzu, who may have lived around the sixth century BC, though scholars debate whether he was a real historical person or a legendary one. The foundational text of Taoism is the Tao Te Ching, a short, poetic book filled with paradoxes and mysterious imagery.

The word "Tao" means "the Way," and it refers to the fundamental principle that underlies all of reality. The Tao is not a god. It is not a person. It is more like the natural order of the universe, the force that keeps rivers flowing downhill, seasons changing, and stars burning in the sky. The Tao Te Ching opens with the famous line, "The Tao that can be told is not the eternal Tao." In other words, the moment you try to pin it down with words, you have already missed it.

Taoism teaches that the best way to live is in harmony with the Tao. This means going with the natural flow of things rather than forcing your will on the world. The Taoist ideal is called wu wei, which is often translated as "non-action" or "effortless action." It does not mean laziness. It means acting in a way that is natural, unforced, and in tune with the way things are. Water is the favorite metaphor in Taoism. Water does not fight. It flows around obstacles, settles in the lowest places, and yet over time it shapes mountains. Taoists say the wisest person is like water.

Taoism also introduced the concept of yin and yang, the idea that reality is made up of complementary opposites: light and dark, hot and cold, active and passive. Neither side is good or evil. Both are necessary. Balance between them is the goal.

Over time, Taoism developed a religious side that went well beyond Lao Tzu's philosophy. Taoist priests, temples, rituals, and a vast collection of gods and spirits became part of Chinese religious life. Practices like feng shui (arranging your environment to promote positive energy) and various forms of fortune telling grew out of the Taoist tradition.

There is something appealing about Taoism's respect for nature and its caution against arrogance. But from a Christian perspective, the Tao is a poor substitute for God. The Tao does not know you. It does not love you. It does not speak. It cannot forgive. It is a principle, not a person. And a universe governed by an impersonal principle is a universe where human beings are ultimately alone, no matter how beautifully the rivers flow.

BUDDHISM IN CHINA

You already studied Buddhism in the previous chapter, so there is no need to cover all the same ground. But it is worth noting how Buddhism changed when it arrived in China. Buddhism entered China from India along trade routes during the first century AD and gradually became one of the three pillars of Chinese religious life.

Chinese Buddhism developed its own flavor. The most significant Chinese contribution was Chan Buddhism, which later became Zen Buddhism when it spread to Japan. Chinese Buddhists also developed a strong tradition of devotion to bodhisattvas, particularly Guanyin, the bodhisattva of compassion, who became one of the most beloved figures in Chinese religion. Temples honoring Guanyin can be found across China to this day.

In Chinese folk religion, Buddhist ideas about karma, rebirth, and the afterlife blended with Confucian ethics and Taoist philosophy to create a worldview that borrows from all three without being fully committed to any one of them.

ANCESTOR VENERATION

If there is one thread that ties all of Chinese traditional religion together, it is ancestor veneration. Across every tradition and every region, honoring the dead has been central to Chinese religious practice for thousands of years.

Chinese families maintain altars or shrines in their homes where they display photographs or tablets representing deceased relatives. They offer food, burn incense, and sometimes burn paper items meant to provide for their ancestors in the afterlife.

Major festivals like Qingming (Tomb Sweeping Day) and the Ghost Festival are dedicated to honoring and caring for the dead.

This practice is rooted in the belief that the dead continue to exist in some form and that they can influence the lives of their living descendants. Keeping the ancestors happy and well-provided-for is seen as both a duty and a practical necessity. Neglecting them could bring misfortune. Honoring them brings blessing and protection.

The Bible certainly teaches respect for parents and gratitude for those who came before us. "Honor your father and your mother" (Exodus 20:12) is one of the Ten Commandments. But there is an important line between honoring the memory of the dead and directing prayers, offerings, and rituals toward them. The Bible teaches that prayer belongs to God alone. The dead cannot hear your prayers, and they do not need your offerings. Ancestor veneration, however well-intentioned, crosses a line that Scripture draws clearly.

THE BLEND IN PRACTICE

What makes Chinese traditional religion hard to pin down is that it is not a system anyone designed. It is a living, breathing cultural reality that has grown over thousands of years. A Chinese family might celebrate the Lunar New Year with firecrackers and offerings to household gods, consult a fortune teller before building a house, teach their children Confucian values of respect and hard work, visit a Buddhist temple to pray for a sick relative, and sweep their ancestors' graves every spring. None of this feels contradictory to them. It all fits together as simply "the way things are done."

From a Christian perspective, this raises a crucial question: Can truth be assembled from pieces of different systems, or does it have to come from one source?

The Bible's answer is clear. God does not present himself as one option among many. "I am the way, and the truth, and the life. No one comes to the Father except through me" (John 14:6). Jesus does not invite you to take his best ideas and blend them with a few teachings from Confucius and a splash of Taoist philosophy. He makes an exclusive claim. Either he is who he says he is, or he is not. But he does not leave room for a buffet-style approach to truth.

That does not mean everything in Chinese traditional religion is wrong. Confucian respect for parents is good. Taoist humility before nature is good. The Buddhist recognition that suffering is real is good. But good ideas scattered across many systems are not the same as the truth revealed by the living God. You do not need to build your own religion from spare parts when the Creator of the universe has already spoken.

WHAT THIS MEANS FOR US

First, truth is not a buffet. The Chinese approach to religion treats beliefs like ingredients you can mix and match. Christianity says truth comes from one source, and that source is God's revealed word. You do not get to pick and choose the parts you like and discard the rest.

Second, good ideas are not enough. Confucian ethics and Taoist wisdom contain genuinely helpful insights. But helpful insights are not the same as saving truth. A religion that helps you be a better neighbor but cannot reconcile you to God has left the biggest problem unsolved.

Third, respect for the dead has limits. Honoring the memory of loved ones who have passed away is right and good. But directing prayers, offerings, or rituals toward the dead is something Scripture does not support. Keep your prayers pointed at the One who can actually hear them.

Fourth, culture shapes religion more than we realize. Chinese traditional religion is a vivid reminder that what people believe is often shaped by the culture they grow up in. That is true for everyone, including Christians. The question to always ask is not "what does my culture teach?" but "what does the Bible teach?"

TALKING POINTS

1. Chinese traditional religion blends Confucianism, Taoism, and Buddhism without treating them as contradictory. Why do you think that approach appeals to so many people? What are the risks of blending different belief systems together?

2. Confucius focused almost entirely on this world and avoided questions about God and the afterlife. What are the strengths of that approach? What are its weaknesses?

3. Taoism teaches that the best life is one lived in harmony with the natural flow of things. How does that compare to the Christian idea of living in obedience to a personal God who speaks and gives specific instructions?

4. Ancestor veneration is deeply important in Chinese culture. How would you explain to a Chinese friend the difference between honoring the memory of someone who has died and directing prayers and offerings to them?

5. Jesus said, "I am the way, and the truth, and the life." How does that exclusive claim challenge the idea that you can build a good religion by combining the best ideas from many different traditions?

Alice eventually found her way out of Wonderland, but she never did figure out how all its pieces fit together. That is because they were never meant to. A world built from mismatched parts may be colorful and fascinating, but it is not a world you can trust with your life. Chinese traditional religion is rich, ancient, and deeply human. But richness and age do not equal truth. The God of the Bible does not ask you to wander through a wonderland of competing philosophies, picking up what looks interesting. He asks you to follow one road, and he promises that it leads home.

Turn the page.

9

SIKHISM

The movie *The Truman Show* follows Truman Burbank, a cheerful insurance salesman who has no idea that his entire life is fake. His town, his neighbors, even the sky above him are all part of an enormous television set. Every person he interacts with is an actor. Every sunrise is controlled by a lighting crew. Truman has been living inside a world that other people built for him, following rules that other people wrote, and he has never once questioned whether any of it is real.

Then cracks begin to appear. A spotlight falls from the sky. A rainstorm follows only him. A woman he loves tries to tell him the truth before she is dragged away. Slowly, Truman starts to suspect that the world he has been handed is not the whole story. And eventually, despite everything designed to keep him inside, he sails to the edge of the set, finds a door in the painted sky, and walks through it.

Truman did not know what was on the other side of that door. He only knew that what was behind him was not enough.

Five hundred years ago, a man in the Punjab region of India came to a similar conclusion. He had grown up surrounded by two massive religious systems, Hinduism and Islam, and he respected elements of both. But after a profound spiritual experience, he became convinced that neither one had the full picture. He did not try to fix them from the inside. He walked through the door and started something new.

His name was Guru Nanak, and the faith he founded is called Sikhism.

GURU NANAK

Nanak was born in 1469 in the village of Talwandi, in the Punjab region of what is now Pakistan. He grew up in a Hindu family but lived in an area with a large Muslim population, so he was exposed to both traditions from an early age. Even as a boy, he showed an unusual interest in spiritual questions and a tendency to challenge the religious customs around him.

The turning point came when Nanak was about thirty years old. According to Sikh tradition, he went to bathe in a river one morning and disappeared for three days. When he returned, he was a changed man. He announced that God had given him a mission, and his first words carried the message that would define Sikhism: "There is no Hindu, there is no Muslim." He did not mean that Hindus and Muslims did not exist. He meant that the divisions people had created between themselves were not what God cared about. True religion, Nanak taught, was about a direct, personal relationship with the one true God, and it had nothing to do with the rituals, caste distinctions, and religious labels that people used to separate themselves from each other.

Nanak spent the rest of his life traveling, teaching, and gathering followers. The word "Sikh" comes from a term meaning “learner” or “disciple.” Nanak became the first in a line of ten Gurus, or spiritual teachers, who shaped the Sikh faith over the next two centuries.

ONE GOD

Like Christianity, Islam, and Judaism, Sikhism is strictly monotheistic. Sikhs believe in one God who created the universe and sustains it. The Sikh symbol Ik Onkar, which means “one God,” is the opening phrase of their most important prayer and the foundation of everything they believe.

But the Sikh understanding of God differs from the Christian one in important ways. The Sikh God is formless, meaning God has no body and takes no physical shape. God is not male or female. God does not become incarnate the way Christians believe Jesus is God in the flesh. God is everywhere, present in all of creation, but God is not a person you can sit down and have a conversation with the way the Bible portrays prayer.

Sikhs also reject the Trinity. For Sikhs, God is absolutely one, with no divisions, no persons, and no son. The idea that God would take on human form is seen as limiting an unlimited being. This puts Sikhism in the same broad camp as Islam and Judaism on the question of God’s nature, though Sikhism arrived at that position independently.

Christianity agrees that God is one and that God is the creator of everything. But the Bible insists that this one God is personal. He speaks. He listens. He enters into covenants. He reveals himself in history. And in Jesus, he enters the world he made in order to rescue the people he loves. A God who cannot be known personally may inspire reverence, but he cannot offer relationship. And relationship, according to the Bible, is the entire point.

THE TEN GURUS

Sikhism was shaped by a succession of ten human Gurus, beginning with Nanak and ending with Guru Gobind Singh, who died in 1708. Each Guru built on the work of those before him, developing Sikh theology, community life, and identity.

Some of the Gurus were teachers and poets. Others were warriors who fought to defend the Sikh community against persecution from the Mughal Empire. Guru Arjan, the fifth Guru, compiled the first official collection of Sikh scriptures. He was also the first Sikh martyr, executed by the Mughal emperor for refusing to convert to Islam. Guru Gobind Singh, the tenth and final human Guru, established the Khalsa, a community of initiated Sikhs who committed themselves to a distinct code of conduct and appearance.

Before he died, Guru Gobind Singh made a decision that set Sikhism apart from most other religions. He declared that there would be no eleventh human Guru. Instead, the Sikh scripture itself would serve as the eternal Guru from that point forward. That scripture is called the Guru Granth Sahib.

THE GURU GRANTH SAHIB

The Guru Granth Sahib is not just a holy book that Sikhs read and study. It is treated as a living presence. In a Sikh place of worship, called a Gurdwara, the Guru Granth Sahib is placed on a special throne, draped in fine cloth, and attended to with a ceremonial fan. It is opened in the morning and put to rest at night. Sikhs bow before it when they enter the room. It is, in a very real sense, the center of Sikh worship and life.

The Guru Granth Sahib contains 1,430 pages of hymns, poems, and prayers composed by the Sikh Gurus as well as several Hindu and Muslim saints whose writings were considered consistent with Sikh teaching. It is written primarily in Gurmukhi script and is always kept in its original language.

New Testament Christians also hold their Scripture in high regard and treat it as the final authority. But there is a difference between respecting the Bible as God's inspired word and treating a physical copy of a book as if it were itself a living being. The Bible points beyond itself to the God who spoke it. The Guru Granth Sahib, in Sikh practice, comes close to being treated as the object of devotion itself.

EQUALITY AND SERVICE

One of the most admirable features of Sikhism is its fierce commitment to equality. Guru Nanak rejected the Hindu caste system and taught that all people are equal in the eyes of God regardless of birth, wealth, gender, or social position. This was a radical message in fifteenth-century India, and it remains central to Sikh identity today.

This commitment shows up most visibly in the practice of langar, a communal meal served at every Gurdwara. Anyone, regardless of religion, race, or background, is welcome to sit on the floor and eat together. The meal is prepared and served by volunteers, and everyone sits at the same level to emphasize that no one is above anyone else. Some of the largest Gurdwaras serve tens of thousands of free meals every single day.

Seva, or selfless service, is another pillar of Sikh life. Sikhs are taught that serving others without expecting anything in return is one of the highest forms of devotion to God. This ethic of service has made Sikh communities known for their generosity around the world, from disaster relief to feeding the homeless.

Christians should recognize something familiar here. Jesus told his followers, "Whoever would be great among you must be your servant" (Matthew 20:26). The values of equality and selfless service are not unique to Sikhism. They are written into the fabric of the gospel. But the motivation matters. In Christianity, service flows from gratitude for what God has already done. You serve because you have been served. In Sikhism, service is part of the path toward God. The direction of the arrow is different, even if the actions look the same.

THE FIVE KS

Initiated Sikhs who are part of the Khalsa community are recognized by five articles of faith, all of which begin with the letter K in the Punjabi language.

Kesh is uncut hair, which represents respect for God's creation as it is. Sikh men typically cover their hair with a turban, which has become one of the most recognizable symbols of the Sikh faith. Kangha is a small wooden comb worn in the hair, symbolizing cleanliness and order. Kara is a steel bracelet worn on the wrist, representing God's eternity and the Sikh's bond to the Guru. Kachera refers to a specific style of undergarment symbolizing self-discipline. Kirpan is a small ceremonial sword or dagger, representing the duty to stand up for justice and protect the weak.

These five articles are not optional accessories for Khalsa Sikhs. They are part of their identity, and wearing them is an act of faith and obedience. For many Sikhs living in Western countries, the kirpan and the turban have occasionally become points of misunderstanding or discrimination. Knowing what these items represent can help you treat Sikh neighbors with the respect and understanding they deserve.

KARMA, REBIRTH, AND SALVATION

Like Hinduism and Buddhism, Sikhism teaches karma and the cycle of rebirth. A person's actions in this life affect what happens in the next. The soul passes through many lifetimes, and the goal is to break free from the cycle.

But Sikhism's path to liberation looks different from both Hinduism and Buddhism. Sikhs believe that liberation comes through devotion to God, specifically through meditating on God's name and living a life of honesty, hard work, and service. The practice of repeating and reflecting on the name of God is central to Sikh spirituality. Sikhs believe that as a person draws closer to God through devotion, God's grace meets them and frees them from the cycle of rebirth.

That mention of grace is worth pausing on. Sikhism is one of the few non-Christian religions that gives grace a significant role. Sikhs do not believe they can earn their way out of the cycle purely by their own effort. God's grace is necessary. This makes Sikhism, in some ways, closer to Christianity than many of the other religions in this book.

But the similarities have limits. Sikh grace does not involve a savior. There is no cross, no sacrifice, no one who steps in to bear the penalty for sin. Sikh grace is more like God choosing to release a devoted person from the cycle when the time is right. In Christianity, grace is tied to a specific event in history: the death and resurrection of Jesus. Grace is not abstract. It has a face, a name, and nail-scarred hands. That specificity is what sets the Christian understanding of grace apart from every other version.

SIKHISM AND CHRISTIANITY

Sikhism and Christianity share more common ground than you might expect. Both are monotheistic. Both reject the caste system and affirm human equality. Both value service, humility, and community. Both acknowledge that human effort alone is not enough and that grace plays a role in salvation.

But the differences are real. Sikhism's God is formless and impersonal. Christianity's God is personal and has made himself known in Jesus. Sikhism's path to God runs through meditation and devotion. Christianity's path runs through the cross. Sikhism teaches reincarnation. Christianity teaches resurrection. Sikhism honors ten human Gurus and a sacred book as the final authority. Christianity points to one Lord and one inspired Scripture that reveals him.

These are not small differences. They are different answers to the biggest questions of all: Who is God? What has he done? And how can we be made right with him?

WHAT THIS MEANS FOR US

First, monotheism is not enough on its own. Sikhism, Islam, Judaism, and Christianity all worship one God. But agreeing that God is one does not mean they are talking about the same being. The character, nature, and actions of God matter as much as the number.

Second, grace without a cross is incomplete. Sikhism's recognition that people need God's grace is closer to the truth than a pure works-based system. But grace has to come from somewhere and cost something. The Christian gospel says grace cost God his Son. That is what gives it weight.

Third, let their service challenge you. The Sikh commitment to feeding the hungry and serving the vulnerable is remarkable and consistent. Christians who claim to follow a servant-King should be at least as generous. If a Sikh community is out-serving your church, that is worth reflecting on.

Fourth, know the difference between respect and agreement. Sikhs are often deeply kind, generous, and sincere people. Their faith has produced communities that genuinely care for others. You can admire those qualities and learn from that example without accepting the theology behind it. Respect the people. Engage the ideas honestly.

TALKING POINTS

1. Guru Nanak said, "There is no Hindu, there is no Muslim." What do you think he meant by that? Do you agree that religious labels can get in the way of knowing God?

2. Sikhism teaches that God is formless and impersonal. Christianity teaches that God is personal and became human in Jesus. Why does it matter whether God can be known personally?

3. The Sikh practice of langar, serving free meals to anyone regardless of background, puts their belief in equality into action.

How well does your church put its beliefs about equality and service into action? What could you learn from the Sikh example?

4. Sikhism gives grace a role in salvation but does not connect it to a savior or a sacrifice. Why do Christians believe that grace requires the cross? What would be missing if you had grace without a sacrifice?

5. Of all the religions you have studied in this book, which one surprised you the most? Which one do you think would be the hardest to discuss with a friend who believed it, and why?

You have traveled a long way since Chapter 1. You started with your own faith, the story of a personal God who created the world, entered it, and gave his life to rescue it. From there you moved outward, circle by circle, through traditions that share pieces of that story but tell it differently, and through traditions that tell an entirely different story altogether. You have visited cathedrals and temples, encountered prophets and gurus, and wrestled with ideas about karma, reincarnation, and the meaning of suffering.

Every religion in this book is an attempt to answer the same handful of questions: Who are we? Why are we here? What has gone wrong? And how do we fix it? The answers vary wildly, but the questions are universal. They are your questions too. And the fact that billions of people across every continent and every century have asked them tells you something important: human beings were made to search for something beyond themselves.

Christianity's claim is that the search has an answer, and the answer is not a philosophy, a path, or a set of rules. The answer is a person. His name is Jesus, and he is not waiting for you to find him. He has already come looking for you.

NOTES

The following notes point you to the original sources behind claims made in this book. If you want to see what a religion teaches in its own words, these references will get you there. Page numbers and editions may vary, but the documents themselves are widely available in print and online.

CHAPTER 2: CATHOLICISM

Three sources of authority (Scripture, Sacred Tradition, and the Magisterium): *Catechism of the Catholic Church*, paragraphs 80–87. The Catechism states that "Sacred Tradition and Sacred Scripture make up a single sacred deposit of the Word of God" (par. 97) and that "the task of giving an authentic interpretation of the Word of God … has been entrusted to the living, teaching office of the Church alone" (par. 85).

The Pope as successor of Peter: *Catechism of the Catholic Church*, paragraphs 880–882. The Catechism teaches that "the Bishop of Rome … has full, supreme, and universal power over the whole Church" (par. 882).

Papal infallibility: The doctrine was formally defined at the First Vatican Council (1870) in the document *Pastor Aeternus*, Chapter 4. The *Catechism of the Catholic Church* restates it in paragraph 891.

The Immaculate Conception of Mary: Defined by Pope Pius IX in the 1854 papal bull *Ineffabilis Deus*. See also *Catechism of the Catholic Church*, paragraph 491.

The perpetual virginity of Mary: *Catechism of the Catholic Church*, paragraph 499.

The Assumption of Mary: Defined by Pope Pius XII in the 1950 apostolic constitution *Munificentissimus Deus*. See also *Catechism of the Catholic Church*, paragraphs 966 and 974.

Praying to Mary and the saints (veneration vs. worship): *Catechism of the Catholic Church*, paragraphs 2673–2679 (on prayer to Mary) and 956–957 (on intercession of the saints).

The seven sacraments: *Catechism of the Catholic Church*, paragraphs 1210–1211 lists all seven: Baptism, Confirmation, Eucharist, Reconciliation, Anointing of the Sick, Holy Orders, and Matrimony.

Purgatory: *Catechism of the Catholic Church*, paragraphs 1030–1032.

Transubstantiation: The term was formally defined at the Fourth Lateran Council (1215) and reaffirmed at the Council of Trent (1551). See *Catechism of the Catholic Church*, paragraphs 1373–1377.

CHAPTER 3: MORMONISM AND JEHOVAH'S WITNESSES

Joseph Smith's First Vision: *Joseph Smith—History* 1:15–20, found in the Pearl of Great Price. Smith describes seeing "two Personages" who told him all existing churches were wrong.

Additional scriptures: The Book of Mormon, the Doctrine and Covenants, and the Pearl of Great Price are all accepted as scripture alongside the Bible. See *Articles of Faith* 1:8 (Pearl of Great Price): "We believe the Bible to be the word of God as far as it is translated correctly; we also believe the Book of Mormon to be the word of God."

God was once a human being: This teaching originates in Joseph Smith's King Follett Discourse (1844). Smith taught: "God himself was once as we are now, and is an exalted man." See also Lorenzo Snow's couplet: "As man now is, God once was; as God now is, man may be." The doctrine is discussed in the LDS manual *Gospel Principles*, Chapter 47 ("Exaltation").

God the Father has a physical body of flesh and bone: *Doctrine and Covenants* 130:22: "The Father has a body of flesh and bones as tangible as man's; the Son also; but the Holy Ghost has not a body of flesh and bones, but is a personage of Spirit."

The Father, Son, and Holy Spirit as three separate gods: *Articles of Faith* 1:1 declares belief in "God, the Eternal Father, and in His Son, Jesus Christ, and in the Holy Ghost" but LDS theology teaches these are three distinct beings. See also *Doctrine and Covenants* 130:22 and *Teachings of the Prophet Joseph Smith*, compiled by Joseph Fielding Smith, pp. 370–372.

Jesus as the firstborn spirit child of the Father; Lucifer as a spirit brother: *Gospel Principles*, Chapter 3: "The first spirit born to our heavenly parents was Jesus Christ." *Moses* 4:1–4

(Pearl of Great Price) and *Abraham* 3:27–28 describe the premortal council where both Jesus and Lucifer presented plans.

Baptism for the dead: *Doctrine and Covenants* 128:15–18. Joseph Smith taught that "the greatest responsibility in this world that God has laid upon us is to seek after our dead."

Temple sealing ceremonies: *Doctrine and Covenants* 132:19–20 describes the "new and everlasting covenant of marriage" performed in temples, which Mormons believe binds families for eternity.

A living prophet leads the church: *Doctrine and Covenants* 1:38: "Whether by mine own voice or by the voice of my servants, it is the same." See also *Doctrine and Covenants* 21:4–5, which instructs members to receive the prophet's word "as if from mine own mouth."

The New World Translation and John 1:1: The *New World Translation of the Holy Scriptures* (published by the Watch Tower Bible and Tract Society) renders John 1:1c as "the Word was a god" rather than "the Word was God." The Watchtower defends this rendering in the appendix of the 1984 edition and in *The Watchtower*, November 1, 2008.

Jesus is Michael the archangel: *Insight on the Scriptures*, Vol. 2, under "Michael," published by the Watch Tower Society. See also *What Does the Bible Really Teach?* (2005), p. 218–219.

The Holy Spirit as God's "active force": *What Does the Bible Really Teach?*, Chapter 15, published by the Watch Tower Society. The book describes the holy spirit as "God's active force" rather than a person.

Only 144,000 go to heaven: *What Does the Bible Really Teach?*, Chapter 7. The Watchtower teaches that 144,000 "anointed" Christians will rule in heaven with Christ, while the "great crowd" will live forever on a paradise earth.

Annihilation of the wicked (no hell): *What Does the Bible Really Teach?*, Chapter 6. The Watchtower teaches that the dead are "conscious of nothing" and that the wicked simply cease to exist.

Disfellowshipping and shunning: *Organized to Do Jehovah's Will* (published by the Watch Tower Society), Chapter 14. See also *The Watchtower*, April 15, 2015, which instructs members to avoid contact with disfellowshipped individuals, including family members.

Failed predictions: The Watch Tower Society predicted significant events for 1914 (*The Time Is at Hand*, 1889), 1925 (*Millions Now Living Will Never Die*, 1920), and 1975 (*Life Everlasting—In Freedom of the Sons of God*, 1966). When these dates passed without the predicted events, the organization revised its interpretations.

CHAPTER 4: JUDAISM

613 commandments in the Torah: The count of 613 commandments (mitzvot) is traditionally attributed to Rabbi Simlai, as recorded in the Babylonian Talmud, Makkot 23b. The most well-known enumeration was compiled by Maimonides in his *Sefer HaMitzvot* (Book of the Commandments) in the twelfth century.

The Shema as the central prayer: Deuteronomy 6:4–9 is the source text. The Shema is recited daily in Jewish worship, as prescribed in the Mishnah, Berakhot 1:1–4.

Jewish interpretation of Isaiah 53 as referring to Israel: This interpretation appears in rabbinic sources including Rashi's commentary on Isaiah 53 (eleventh century) and is the most widely held Jewish reading of the passage.

Branches of Judaism: For an overview of the distinctions between Orthodox, Conservative, and Reform Judaism, see the respective movements' own statements of principles: the Orthodox Union (ou.org), the United Synagogue of Conservative Judaism (uscj.org), and the Union for Reform Judaism (urj.org).

CHAPTER 5: ISLAM

The Quran as God's literal word dictated through Gabriel: Surah 2:97 identifies Gabriel (Jibril) as the one who delivered the Quran. The belief that the Quran is God's literal, uncreated word is a core Islamic doctrine, articulated in virtually every introduction to Islamic theology. See also Surah 26:192–195.

Abraham commanded to sacrifice Ishmael: The Quran tells the story of the sacrifice in Surah 37:99–113 without naming the son. Islamic tradition identifies the son as Ishmael, as reflected in the writings of scholars like Ibn Kathir in his *Tafsir* (commentary on the Quran) on Surah 37:102.

The Five Pillars of Islam: These are drawn from multiple Quranic passages and from the Hadith. The most concise statement is found in Sahih al-Bukhari, Book 2, Hadith 8 (also known as the Hadith of Gabriel), where Muhammad lists the five pillars. Shahada: Surah 3:18. Salat: Surah 2:238, Surah 11:114. Zakat: Surah 2:43. Sawm: Surah 2:183–185. Hajj: Surah 3:97.

Tawhid (the absolute oneness of God): Surah 112 (Al-Ikhlas) is the definitive statement: "Say, 'He is Allah, [who is] One.

Allah, the Eternal Refuge. He neither begets nor is born, nor is there to Him any equivalent.'"

Shirk as the one unforgivable sin: Surah 4:48: "Indeed, Allah does not forgive association with Him, but He forgives what is less than that for whom He wills."

Islam's denial of the crucifixion: Surah 4:157–158: "They did not kill him, nor did they crucify him; but [another] was made to resemble him to them … rather, Allah raised him to Himself."

Islam's denial that Jesus is the Son of God: Surah 4:171: "Christ Jesus, the son of Mary, was but a messenger of Allah … So believe in Allah and His messengers. And do not say, 'Three'; desist — it is better for you. Indeed, Allah is but one God."

No concept of original sin in Islam: This is a widely held Islamic position. The Quran teaches that Adam sinned but was forgiven (Surah 2:37: "Then Adam received from his Lord [some] words, and He accepted his repentance"). Islamic theology does not extend Adam's sin to his descendants. See also Surah 53:38: "No bearer of burdens will bear the burden of another."

Judgment by weighing deeds on a scale: Surah 21:47: "And We place the scales of justice for the Day of Resurrection, so no soul will be treated unjustly at all." See also Surah 7:8–9 and Surah 101:6–11.

Muhammad's uncertainty about his own eternal fate: Sahih al-Bukhari, Hadith 3929 (also recorded as 1243 and 7003 in the same collection). Muhammad is reported to have said: "By Allah, though I am the Apostle of Allah, yet I do not know what Allah will do to me."

Sunni/Shia split: The dispute over succession is documented in early Islamic histories, particularly Ibn Hisham's recension of Ibn Ishaq's *Sirat Rasul Allah* (Life of the Messenger of God), one of the earliest biographies of Muhammad.

CHAPTER 6: HINDUISM

Brahman as the ultimate, impersonal reality: The Upanishads are the primary source. The Chandogya Upanishad 3.14.1 describes Brahman as "all this." The Mundaka Upanishad 2.2.11 declares "Brahman is all." See also the Brihadaranyaka Upanishad 3.9.28.

Brahma, Vishnu, and Shiva (the Trimurti): The concept of the three primary manifestations of Brahman appears across multiple texts. See the Vishnu Purana, Book 1, Chapter 2, for a description of creation, preservation, and destruction.

Vishnu's ten avatars, including Rama and Krishna: The list of ten avatars (Dashavatara) is found in multiple Puranas, most notably the Garuda Purana 1.86.10–11 and the Bhagavata Purana, Canto 1, Chapter 3.

Karma as moral cause and effect: The Brihadaranyaka Upanishad 4.4.5: "According as one acts, according as one behaves, so does he become." See also the Bhagavad Gita 18.12.

Samsara (the cycle of rebirth): The Bhagavad Gita 2.22 uses the well-known analogy: "As a person puts on new garments, giving up old ones, the soul similarly accepts new material bodies, giving up the old and useless ones."

Moksha (liberation): The Bhagavad Gita 8.15–16 describes moksha as reaching the "supreme destination" from which one does not return to the cycle of rebirth. The

Mundaka Upanishad 3.2.8–9 describes the soul merging with Brahman.

Three paths to moksha: Jnana yoga (knowledge): discussed in the Upanishads, especially the Brihadaranyaka Upanishad. Bhakti yoga (devotion): articulated in the Bhagavad Gita 9.26–34 and 12.1–12. Karma yoga (selfless action): discussed in the Bhagavad Gita 3.4–9.

The four varnas (caste system): The Rigveda 10.90 (the Purusha Sukta) is the earliest source, describing the four groups as originating from different parts of the cosmic being. The Laws of Manu (Manusmriti), Chapter 1, verses 87–91, provides a more detailed description of the duties of each varna.

CHAPTER 7: BUDDHISM

The Four Noble Truths: The Buddha's first sermon, known as the Dhammacakkappavattana Sutta ("Setting the Wheel of Dharma in Motion"), is found in the Pali Canon, Samyutta Nikaya 56.11. This is the foundational text for the Four Noble Truths.

The Eightfold Path: Also found in the Dhammacakkappavattana Sutta (Samyutta Nikaya 56.11). A more detailed treatment appears in the Magga-vibhanga Sutta (Samyutta Nikaya 45.8).

Buddhism does not require belief in God: The Buddha's pragmatic silence on the question of God is illustrated in several texts, most notably the Cula-Malunkyovada Sutta (Majjhima Nikaya 63), often called "the Parable of the Poisoned Arrow," in which the Buddha refuses to answer metaphysical questions and focuses instead on the practical problem of suffering.

Nirvana as "blowing out": The word nibbana (Pali) or nirvana (Sanskrit) literally means "extinguishing" or "blowing out." The cessation of craving as the path to nirvana is taught in the Dhammacakkappavattana Sutta (Samyutta Nikaya 56.11), where the Third Noble Truth describes "the remainderless fading and cessation" of craving. The term and its meaning are discussed across multiple Pali Canon texts, including the Itivuttaka 38, which describes nirvana as the destruction of greed, hatred, and delusion.

No permanent self (anatta): The doctrine of "no-self" is taught in the Anattalakkhana Sutta (Samyutta Nikaya 22.59), the Buddha's second sermon.

Karma and rebirth without a permanent soul: The candle-flame analogy (consciousness transferred without a permanent self) is a common teaching illustration drawn from the Milindapanha ("Questions of King Milinda"), a classical Buddhist text, Chapter 3.

Theravada, Mahayana, and Zen: The distinctions between these branches are described in numerous scholarly introductions to Buddhism. For primary Mahayana texts introducing the bodhisattva ideal, see the Lotus Sutra (Saddharma Pundarika Sutra), Chapters 2–4. For Zen, the foundational text is the Platform Sutra of the Sixth Patriarch (Liu Zu Tan Jing).

CHAPTER 8: CHINESE TRADITIONAL AND FOLK RELIGIONS

Confucius on spirits and death: The Analects of Confucius, Book 11, Chapter 12 (11.12): "If you are not able to serve man, how can you serve the spirits? … If you do not know about life, how can you know about death?"

The five key relationships: The Analects of Confucius, various passages, especially Book 1. The classic formulation of the "Five Bonds" (wu lun) is found in the Mencius (Mengzi), Book 3A, Chapter 4.

Filial piety: The Analects, Book 1, Chapters 2, 6, and 11 emphasize the centrality of filial piety. The Classic of Filial Piety (Xiaojing) is a short Confucian text devoted entirely to this virtue.

The Tao Te Ching opening line: Tao Te Ching (attributed to Lao Tzu), Chapter 1: "The Tao that can be told is not the eternal Tao."

Wu wei (non-action or effortless action): Tao Te Ching, Chapters 2, 37, 43, and 48. Chapter 43 states: "The softest thing in the universe overcomes the hardest thing in the universe."

Yin and yang: The concept appears throughout classical Chinese philosophy. Its earliest systematic treatment is found in the I Ching (Book of Changes), one of the oldest Chinese texts, and in the writings of Zou Yan (third century BC).

Chan Buddhism becoming Zen: The Bodhidharma tradition and the development of Chan (Zen) Buddhism in China are recorded in texts such as the Jingde Record of the Transmission of the Lamp (Jingde Chuandeng Lu), compiled in 1004 AD.

CHAPTER 9: SIKHISM

Guru Nanak's declaration: "There is no Hindu, there is no Muslim": This statement is attributed to Guru Nanak after his three-day disappearance at the river Bein. It is recorded in the Janam Sakhis (traditional biographical accounts of Guru

Nanak's life), the most well-known being the Puratan Janam Sakhi and the Bala Janam Sakhi.

Ik Onkar ("one God"): The Guru Granth Sahib opens with the Mool Mantar (Root Mantra), which begins: "Ik Onkar, Sat Naam, Karta Purakh …" ("One God, True Name, Creator Being …"). This appears on page 1 of the Guru Granth Sahib.

Guru Arjan as the first Sikh martyr: Guru Arjan's martyrdom in 1606 is recorded in Sikh historical sources including the Gurbilas Patshahi 5 and the writings of Bhai Gurdas (a contemporary of Guru Arjan). The Tuzuk-i-Jahangiri (the memoirs of Emperor Jahangir) also references Guru Arjan's execution, though it attributes it to political rather than religious motives.

Guru Gobind Singh established the Khalsa: The creation of the Khalsa in 1699 is recorded in multiple Sikh historical texts, including the Sau Sakhi and the Gurbilas Patshahi 10.

The Guru Granth Sahib as the eternal Guru: Guru Gobind Singh's declaration that the scripture would serve as the final Guru is recorded in Sikh tradition and affirmed by the Shiromani Gurdwara Parbandhak Committee (SGPC), the central authority for Sikh Gurdwaras. The Guru Granth Sahib was given its final form and installed as eternal Guru at Nanded in 1708.

The Guru Granth Sahib contains 1,430 pages and includes writings by Hindu and Muslim saints: The Guru Granth Sahib includes compositions by Guru Nanak and the subsequent Gurus as well as fifteen bhagats (saints) from Hindu and Muslim traditions, including Kabir, Farid, Namdev, and Ravidas. See the table of contents of any standard edition of the Guru Granth Sahib.

The Five Ks: The Sikh Rehat Maryada (Sikh Code of Conduct), published by the SGPC, defines the five articles of faith required for Khalsa Sikhs: Kesh, Kangha, Kara, Kachera, and Kirpan. See Section 4, Chapter 10, Article 16.

Langar (communal meal): The practice of langar is rooted in the teachings of Guru Nanak and was formalized by Guru Angad (the second Guru) and Guru Amar Das (the third Guru). The Sikh Rehat Maryada affirms langar as an essential practice of every Gurdwara.

Grace (nadar/kirpa) in Sikh theology: The Guru Granth Sahib speaks frequently of God's grace. The Japji Sahib (the opening prayer of the Guru Granth Sahib, composed by Guru Nanak), stanza 4, states: "By His Grace, we are redeemed." See also the Mool Mantar (page 1 of the Guru Granth Sahib), which describes God as "Gurprasad" (known by the Guru's grace).

www.ingramcontent.com/pod-product-compliance
Ingram Content Group UK Ltd.
Pitfield, Milton Keynes, MK11 3LW, UK
UKHW020420250726
13967UKWH00007B/2735